40
days in

1 SAMUEL

Titles in 40 Days Series

**40
days in**

1 SAMUEL

DUANE GARRETT

—— *edited by* ——

WILLIAM F. COOK III

B&H
PUBLISHING
NASHVILLE, TENNESSEE

Contents

Preface

Forty is an important number in the Bible. Moses was on Mount Sinai with the Lord God for forty days (Exod. 34:28), Elijah traveled for forty days before arriving at Mount Horeb (1 Kings 19:3–8), and Jesus was tempted in the wilderness for forty days (Mark 1:13). Some self-help experts believe it takes forty days to develop a habit. Whether they're right or wrong, there is no habit more important for a Christian to develop than a consistent devotional life.

In *40 Days in the Word*, readers will discover a humble attempt to assist believers longing for a fresh moving of God's Spirit in their life. This series intends to enable believers to read though books of the Bible in their devotional time discovering God's truth within its biblical context. The Spirit of God uses the Word of God to mature believers in their faith and increase their passion and zeal for Jesus Christ.

Many Christians find it difficult to sustain momentum in their devotional life. They desire to read the Bible consistently but lack encouragement, guidance, and direction. Commentaries are often too technical, and devotionals may fail to challenge them to dig deeply into God's Word. The *40 Days* series offers both a deeper discussion of a biblical passage and encouragement for the reader to make personal applications based upon what the text *actually* says.

We live in a day where casual Christianity (which is not biblical Christianity at all!) has infected the church in the West. People are clamoring for shorter sermons that are more focused on felt-needs rather than on the Bible, and many in the pulpits are obliging. Furthermore, the songs that are often sung fail to extol the greatness of God, but instead make people feel better about themselves and their comfortable lifestyles.

If the church in the West is to recapture the passion of the early church, God's people must spend time on their knees with their Bibles open, allowing God's Spirit to convict them of their sin, build them up in their faith, and empower them to take the gospel across the street and around the world. The hope of the authors of this series is that God's Spirit will use these volumes to help God's people develop an ever-increasing love for their Savior, Jesus Christ.

In addition to helping individual believers, the series holds out hope for small groups desiring to focus their meetings on the study of the Bible. A group would spend approximately two months (five days of readings per week) reading through a book of the Bible along with the *40 Days* volume, and then base their discipleship time encouraging each other with what they discovered during the previous week.

The Spirit of God and the Word of God work together to strengthen God's church. The apostle Paul put it this way: "Let the word of Christ dwell richly among you, in all wisdom teaching and admonishing one another through psalms, hymns, and spiritual songs, singing to God with gratitude in your hearts" (Col. 3:16). Paul's hope is my prayer for you as you journey through these next forty days.

Bill Cook
Holy Week, 2020

Hannah's Prayer

1 Samuel 1:1–28

The Big Picture

As 1 Samuel begins, Israel is a loose confederation of tribes that were sporadically under the leadership of warriors we call the "judges." Israel had no central government and no capital city. There was no regular succession of judges. Individual judges arose and were recognized in times of crisis, as called by Yahweh, and it seems that the authority of any given judge rarely extended far beyond his own tribe. There was no temple; Israel worshiped at the Tent of Meeting, which was set up at Shiloh. The first thing we read is the account of the birth and calling of the last and greatest judge, Samuel.

Digging In

Hannah's anguish over her inability to bear children is understandable to any woman who longs for children and cannot have them. But for an ancient Israelite, the distress was especially severe. Israel had no social safety net whatsoever. There was no provision for a pension, for health care, or public assistance of any kind. If a woman's husband

1

predeceased her, she depended entirely on her children, particularly her sons, to provide for her in old age. Absent that, she might very well starve, and she would certainly have to beg. Charitable giving was entirely a private matter; there was no state to enforce it. When Hannah's husband, Elkanah, asked, "Am I not better to you than ten sons?" he was not making an ego-centric claim that she should be thrilled to have such a fine husband. He was stating that he provided for her generously (he gave her a double portion). While there is no doubt that he did love her and gave her all she needed—and he did not neglect her because she was barren—from her perspective there was still a major problem. If Elkanah predeceased Hannah, the son of Hannah's rival, Peninnah, would be the heir of the estate. Peninnah could then eject Hannah from the household, leaving her destitute.

In addition, there was great cultural pressure for women to have children. A woman who bore no children would probably be regarded as a failure and a disgrace—especially by other women, just as men would despise a man who fled from a battle or who did not properly work his land. For Hannah, her condition meant that she had not fulfilled her role as a woman and was at risk of losing everything. We should not judge her by modern, Western standards.

We read that the priest Eli noticed Hannah because her lips were moving but made no sound (1 Sam. 1:13). We might think that she would have been expected to pray silently, with her mouth shut. In fact, it appears that people in the ancient world always prayed aloud; they did not pray in their minds alone. Thus, what was strange to Eli was that she made no audible words, and thus he thought that she was just a distraught drunk mumbling incoherently. Hannah denied that she was drunk and spoke of her great despair, implying she was so upset she could hardly make her voice work while she prayed.

Eli saw the truth in this and pronounced a blessing over her, telling her she could depart "in peace." A priest is someone who stands between God and other people to serve as an intermediary and intercessor on their behalf. As the high priest, Eli had authority from God to pronounce a blessing over people in Yahweh's name. This did not mean that his blessings were always efficacious; he did not have a superpower. He did, however, speak as God's representative, and Hannah received his words with faith and gratitude, and it gave her peace. In fact, God heard Hannah's prayer and Eli's blessing, and she became pregnant.

Hannah named her son Samuel after he was born, saying, "I requested him from the LORD." We do not, in fact, know what the name "Samuel" means. It sounds somewhat like the Hebrew for "God heard" or for "requested," but it does not actually mean either of these. Whatever the name meant to Hannah, she felt it was an appropriate name for a boy whom she conceived in answer to prayer.

Samuel stayed with his mother until he was weaned. In the ancient world, this could last for a long time, even until a child was between five and seven years of age. We have ancient statuary in which a standing child is nursed by his standing mother. Thus, we should not suppose that when Samuel went to stay with Eli at Shiloh, he was little more than a crawling infant.

Hannah kept the vows she had made about Samuel. First, he was a Nazirite, meaning that during the period of his vow he did not have his hair cut, and he stayed away from whatever would defile him in a ritual sense (such as touching a dead body). The Bible does not elsewhere speak of Samuel as a Nazirite; it may be that she kept him under a Nazirite vow only while he lived with her. Normally, a Nazirite vow was temporary, but we should also see Samuel as a contrast to Samson, the previous judge, who was also a Nazirite but was far less faithful than Samuel. Second, she said that Samuel would stay with Yahweh all his life. Obviously, Hannah could not control what Samuel would do when he was a grown man. What she meant was that she would commit him to Yahweh's service as soon as possible, right after he was weaned. This was a great sacrifice on her part. By surrendering her son to service in the sanctuary, she would release him from his commitment to take care of her. If she had no other sons, she would again face the prospect of poverty. Thus, her vow was a great step of faith.

Living It Out

This passage holds several lessons for us. First, Hannah's distress and subsequent prayer reminds us that we should take our problems to

God and not assume that our mundane troubles do not interest him. Hannah suffered disgrace and reproach and feared falling into poverty. We, too, should cast all our worries on God (1 Pet. 5:7). Second, Eli's blessing over Hannah is a model for what a priest should do: Invoke God's blessing upon other people. Some people speak of the "universal priesthood of the believer" as though it has something to do with freedom of conscience in doctrinal matters. That is not the point at all; it means that we can go directly to God on behalf of others. For Christians, the power to invoke God's blessing on someone is not reserved to an exclusive, ordained priesthood, but it is wasted on us if we do not bless others and intercede for them. Third, Hannah's dedication of her son to God's service, as an act of faith, is a model for us. While we should be careful about making vows (Eccles. 5:4–5), God does desire us to step out in faith and not cling to worldly security.

Hannah's Praise

1 Samuel 2:1–10

The Big Picture

We sometimes think of a psalm strictly as one of the 150 chapters of the book of Psalms, but in fact, one can find many psalms in other books. Hannah's song of praise is such a psalm, and this event, a woman singing a psalm as an expression of her faith in Yahweh, would have been to an ancient Israelite a normal part of religious life. David was the most famous psalmist of Israel, but he was not the only one, and he was not the first. In fact, the psalms we have in the Bible represent only a tiny fraction of the psalms people sang through the history of ancient Israel. Most of them were never written down, just as most of our prayers are never written down.

Hannah composed this psalm to give thanks to God for answered prayer. Even though it was her own composition, it was not entirely original. If you read the Psalms, you will see that they reuse many ideas several times, and sometimes one psalm will repeat phrases verbatim that are found in other psalms. Thus, one did not need to be highly gifted in composition to "create" a new psalm. Much of the psalm composition would be a matter of mixing and matching words and concepts that were part of the standard repertoire of psalms. Finally, although we do not know much about ancient Israelite music, it appears that they were sung to a fairly simple chant. For that reason, an ordinary person could sing a psalm (and all psalms were sung) without being a skilled or trained singer. We should not be surprised that Hannah created and sang a psalm in thanks for the grace she had received; for a pious Israelite woman, it was the normal thing to do.

Digging In

For us, perhaps the most remarkable thing about Hannah's prayer is what she does not say: She never says, "I thank you, God, for giving me a son." This does not mean that she was not grateful for the fact that God answered her earlier prayer and allowed her to have a son. Clearly, she was grateful for this, and she probably voiced her thanks in other, more specific and private prayers. Psalms, however, are almost always general and non-specific. David often prays for deliverance from his enemies in the Psalms, but it is often unclear who these enemies were and what precisely they were doing. Often, we have very little information about what problem David specifically prays about in his psalms. Was he sick? Were his enemies closing in, or was it something else? We often don't know. In the great psalm of confession, Psalm 51, David never mentions that he had committed adultery with Bathsheba and murdered Uriah (we only know that this is in the background of the psalm because of the heading, called a "superscript," at the top of the psalm).

The fact that the Psalms (including Hannah's psalm) are non-specific is of great advantage to us as readers. It allows us to read and pray the psalms in our situation and apply the words of the psalm to our needs, sorrows, and joys. If the psalms were specific, they would be of historical interest but would be of much less value as texts of prayer and praise for us. Anyone, male or female, who has experienced answers to prayer and God's help can pray Hannah's psalm. It is not just for women who had been barren and who now have a baby.

Hannah's psalm is in four parts, as follows: opening praise to Yahweh (1 Sam. 2:1–2); exhortations against arrogant behavior (2:3–5); how Yahweh responds to arrogance and to humility (2:6–9); Yahweh's future work of judgment and salvation (2:10).

The opening praise begins with Hannah's joy in Yahweh (v. 1), and then proceeds to describe the greatness of Yahweh (v. 2). This may seem logically backward, as if we should assert first that God is great and then describe how we love him. But the Old Testament is often very personal, focusing on how humans feel and react first and then moving to theological concepts. That is what gives it such great appeal. Hannah says her heart exults, her horn is raised, and her mouth opens against her enemies (the NRSV translates "horn" as "strength" and translates "opens" as "derides"). The "heart" is the mind and personality; her whole being rejoices in God. The "horn" is a metaphor taken from how a ram or bull raises high its horns as a show of power and confidence; Hannah feels that God has given her great power and a victory. Her mouth is "open" in that she is not put to shame and silenced but can boast in God before all who hate her. Hannah did not necessarily have a large number of personal enemies (although her rival-wife Peninnah no doubt hated her). But language about one's "enemies" is common in psalms; it is a literary motif. It describes anyone who might despise those who fear God. Hannah can rejoice because God has vindicated her.

Verse 2 says there is no "Holy One" like Yahweh (NRSV). The other holy beings could be angels, but it is more likely that it refers to the gods of the nations. The Old Testament will often describe the other gods as though they were real for the purpose of making a comparison to Yahweh. For example, Exodus 15:11 says, "LORD, who is like you among the gods?" The nations have no one like Yahweh to turn to. Hannah then says there is "no one besides you," indicating that the other gods do not exist at all. She finally says Yahweh is her incomparable "rock," meaning that no other god offers such safety.

In her exhortations against arrogant behavior (2:3–5), Hannah talks directly to her audience—those of us who hear or read her words. Psalms are not private prayers or meditations; they are given so that other people can learn from them. She tells us to avoid arrogant behavior and attitudes, warning us that God knows all and carefully weighs all our actions. Again, focusing on human experience, she then gives us three examples of what has befallen people who either did or did not heed her warning (vv. 4–5). Mighty warriors have suffered defeat (because of their arrogance), but physically weak people won victories (if in humility they sought God's help). Rich people (who thought they did not need God) fell into poverty, but the poor (who trusted in God rather than wealth) never went hungry. A barren woman finds herself with a household full of children, but a woman who gave birth to many sons finds herself with no children to care for her. This last example obviously ties to Hannah's own experience, in that she prayed to God for a son, but even so, her psalm is not meant to be read as autobiographical. This idea—that God gives children to the barren but leaves the arrogant woman with many sons destitute—is a biblical motif for how God exalts the lowly and humbles the proud (Isa. 54:1).

When Hannah describes how Yahweh responds with hostility to arrogance but with compassion to humility (1 Sam. 2:6–10a), she asserts that it is not blind fate or "karma" that balances the scales. It is God who brings down the proud and exalts those that turn from their brokenness to him. We serve a living God, and we should take our fears to him. Also, Hannah's psalm effectively equates pride with wickedness. In the Bible, the fear of God comes out of true humility and leads to a devout and upright life.

In her account of Yahweh's future work of judgment and salvation (2:10), Hannah first declares simply that God is great and will judge the wicked and then says he will give strength to his "king" and "anointed." But when Hannah prayed, there was no king in Israel. This is what marks her psalm as truly inspired, just like the psalms of David. She foresaw that God's great work of salvation would be in the anointed king. Although this was fulfilled in a limited way in David, we should remember that the word for "anointed" in Hebrew also means "Messiah."

Living It Out

Hannah exhorts those of us who are doing well to humble ourselves and those of us who are suffering to turn to God. A broken heart can drive us to God, but prosperity can drive us from him. It is harder for a rich man to enter the kingdom of heaven than for a camel to go through the eye of a needle (Matt. 19:24).

Samuel's Childhood at Shiloh

1 Samuel 2:11–36

The Big Picture

Ideally, the time of the judges should have been characterized by maximum virtue and maximum freedom in society, as the nation was ruled not by any human government but by God himself. There would have been no central government to oppress and exploit the people. In this ideal, the people would have lived in an ordered and prudent manner, not being subject to any human laws but, rather, to the Law of God, the Torah. The people, however, would not obey the Torah and served idols instead of the living God. They thus became corrupt and lawless; and wherever some kind of authority did exist, as it did in the priesthood at the Tent of Meeting, there was great corruption and exploitation (the Tent of Meeting was Israel's national religious shrine, the precursor to Solomon's temple). Things had to change. A people who would not submit to God as their king would need to have a human king over them. The current regime at the Tent would have to go, and another priestly family would have to take their place. First Samuel tells the story of these two events. First, it describes the end of the former priestly line at the Tent, and second, it tells of the rise of the monarchy. Today's reading tells us why the old leadership at the shrine had to be purged. ·

Digging In

The boy Samuel remained at the shrine at Shiloh to act as a "hierodule" (a servant in a temple or shrine) under the authority of the High Priest Eli; he was consecrated for lifelong service to Yahweh. This should have been a wonderful environment; it was the place dedicated to the praise of God. But instead, it was a place of great corruption. Samuel grew up seeing wickedness in the house of God on a daily basis.

In 1 Samuel 2:13, we see what had become a normal practice at the shrine: when people offered a sacrifice, a priest's assistant would plunge a fork into the pot boiling the meat and whatever came up was the priest's portion. This policy was, we assume, adopted to make it fair; the cut of meat was randomly selected, and the priest could not pick the best piece for himself. But even this was not in accord with the Torah (see Lev. 10:14–15). What they actually did at this time, however, was much worse. Before the sacrifice was complete (which involved burning fat from the animal before Yahweh as a "pleasing aroma"; see Lev. 17:6), the priest's assistant would demand the choicest cuts of the raw meat for his master. This was disrespectful to the worshipers and showed disdain for God. Even the laypeople knew that the ceremony required the fat to be burned first, but the priests disregarded this and threatened the people with violence if they did not comply (in the ancient world, people regarded fatty cuts of meat as the very best, and that is why the priests took their share before any fat was burned).

For all this, the boy Samuel thrived in his environment. Hannah did not forget her firstborn but took care to bring him a new cloak every year (as all clothing was handmade from raw wool or flax fiber, this represented considerable effort on her part). God also answered her initial fear of being left childless many times over; she had three other sons and two daughters. She was, as an Israelite would have judged it, a richly blessed woman. This is the last time Hannah appears in the narrative.

In 1 Samuel 2:22–26 we read of two different reputations that swirled about the Tent. The people knew that Eli's sons did far worse things than pilfering choice meat. They used the women who served at the shrine as their personal harem, having sex with them as they chose. We do not know much about these women; apparently young, unmarried women were regularly appointed to serve for a period at the shrine (see Num. 6:2; Exod. 38:8). They apparently took care of routine duties involving cleaning, laundry, cooking, and the like; they do not seem to have had any priestly duties. But they were not cult prostitutes, as might be found in a shrine of Baal, and still Eli's sons treated them as such. Eli's rebuke sounds feeble, but his words were true, and the sons bore responsibility for their actions. By contrast, everyone who came to the shrine regarded Samuel to be a young man of exemplary virtue and piety.

In verses 27–34, we read a message given by an anonymous prophet against Eli and his sons. Some readers are surprised that he says that God chose Eli's family to serve as priests while Israel was still in Egypt, but in fact, the Levites already had what we might call "clergy" status before the exodus. Despite what some think, the Levites did not become priests because of their faithfulness at the golden calf incident in Exodus 32:25–29; it is clear from Exodus 29 that the house of Aaron was already regarded as the priestly family. Eli's line was one of several lines descended from Aaron, but not the only one. We do not fully understand the history of the Israelite priesthood (the Old Testament only gives us brief, sideways glances at that story), but this text implies that Eli was of the family line that inherited the right to serve as high priests. There were other Levitical priests, but Eli was in the family line of the high priests. They forfeited the right to continue to hold that office, however, and God chose another Levitical line to take their place.

Verses 35–36 do not name the "faithful priest" who was chosen to replace Eli. The subsequent story suggests that it was Zadok, a priest who was elevated to his high position first by David and then by Solomon (2 Sam. 15:24–36; 1 Kings 1:32–45; 2:35; 1 Chron. 29:22). The prophecy also anticipates the reign of David, saying that this priest would "walk before my anointed," an apparent reference to David. As for the descendants of Eli, they would lose the high priesthood but not the priestly status. They could still serve in the sanctuary if the "faithful priest" would allow them to do so.

Living It Out

Christian ministers, like Israel's priests, can be just as corrupt as the society around them. Sometimes, they are even worse. The behavior of Hannah and Elkanah, however, demonstrates that those who know God will continue to worship him at the sanctuary even though they know that not all is as it should be. For us, that means that we should not abandon the church just because some ministers have proven to have feet of clay. Just as God rewarded faithful Hannah, he will also care for his people today who shine as lights in a corrupt world—or even in a corrupt church. God will deal with corrupt ministers. The house of Eli lost its place of preeminence, and all ministers who defile the church through their behavior will ultimately be exposed and expelled.

Samuel's Calling

1 Samuel 3:1–4:1a

The Big Picture

The shrine of Yahweh, the "Tent of Meeting," resided at Shiloh. This was at the end of the period of the judges, which, as the book of Judges tells us, was a highly decadent time. Israel disregarded God's commands against idolatry and fell into what may be fairly called moral anarchy. This probably explains the statement in verse 1, "In those days the word of the LORD was rare and prophetic visions were not widespread." There were very few genuine prophets of God, and the priests, as is apparent from the behavior of Eli's sons, were thoroughly corrupt. There was a great gulf between the people and God, and for that reason, God rarely gave them any messages.

This is not to say that there were none at all. We saw in 1 Samuel 2:27–36 that a "man of God" came to Eli and pronounced a prophecy of judgment against his house. We should not assume, however, that this event took place while the boy Samuel was serving in the Tent. Eli was already very old by the time Samuel came to serve him, and Eli's sons were well into adulthood. As such, the message from the anonymous prophet of 2:27–36 could have arrived some twenty years before God spoke to Samuel. For all we know, from the time of the anonymous prophet's message to Eli until God spoke to Samuel, God may have sent Israel no messages at all. But Samuel, like his mother Hannah, faithfully served Yahweh. So, it was to this young man that God began again to speak.

Digging In

In verse 2, Eli was lying down in his sleeping chamber, indicating that it was night. It is surprising that the narrative tells us that his eyesight was very poor; he was probably what we would call legally blind. We are probably to understand from this that Eli had become heavily dependent upon Samuel. For this reason, Samuel had become very alert to any call from Eli and was now a light sleeper, with his ears open to any summons from his master.

It is especially surprising that Samuel slept inside the sanctuary of the Tent of Meeting. The Tent (and later, the temple) was divided into two main chambers, a front room called the "holy place" (which contained a table for making bread offerings, an altar for burning incense, and the menorah), and a back room called the "most holy place" (which contained the ark of the covenant). Verse 3 probably means that Samuel slept in the outer chamber, the "holy place" (the clause "where the ark of God was located" describes the entire sanctuary, not the room in which Samuel slept). But even the "holy place" was most sacred; it was where priests performed their rituals of worship. Possibly the main reason Samuel slept there was to tend the menorah, making sure that its lamps burned through the night (Exod. 27:20–21). Even so, it is odd that a servant would sleep in this holy chamber. This may be another example of how careless the priests had become about matters of holiness. In the next chapter, we see that the ark was taken out to a battle, something that should never have happened, and so it is clear that the priests were not scrupulously observant about such things. On the other hand, it was perhaps appropriate that Samuel was in the sanctuary when he heard God's voice.

The point that the lamp had not yet gone out probably means, on a simple, literal level, that the event took place shortly before dawn (the lamps of the menorah were kept burning from dusk to dawn).

Metaphorically, it may imply that although many people, including the priestly leadership, were without God's light (symbolized by Eli's blindness), there were still some who remained faithful to God, such as Samuel.

The Bible relates, in close detail, God's call of Samuel, repeatedly telling how God called Samuel and how Samuel ran to Eli but was told to go back to bed. Besides being a great narrative, this makes the point that God persistently and patiently called Samuel until he got an answer. The very first message Samuel received was a prophecy, a reaffirmation of the word given by the anonymous prophet of chapter 2. This tells the reader that the boy Samuel is now God's prophet. Many years later, God would call the boy Jeremiah to be a prophet (Jer. 1:6–7; Jeremiah was from Anathoth, close to Samuel's hometown of Ramah, and like Samuel he prophesied in a time of upheaval and destruction).

The prophecy affirmed that Eli's family was about to fall in a terrible disaster. Because they had not repented, sacrifices would do them no good. For us, similarly, claims that we have faith in God and the gospel are pointless if we refuse to turn from our sin. Eli, however, is truly a tragic figure. He was not a godless reprobate, as his sons were, and he bravely faced and graciously received God's judgment against him. His sins were not sins of commission (he did not participate in the depravity of his sons), they were sins of omission (he did not expel his sons from priestly service). He was a true worshiper of Yahweh, but his failure to defrock his sons was an affront to God.

Inevitably, Samuel's prophecy came to the attention of "all Israel" (1 Sam. 4:1a). Eli's sons had publicly disgraced the priesthood, and the denunciation of Eli's house was equally public. The public then waited to see if Samuel's words would come true. This would fix in the minds of the people the reputation of both Samuel as God's prophet and of Eli's family line as repudiated by God.

Living It Out

No one lives in an ideal environment. The world seems to get more corrupt every day, and the church is filled with hypocrisy. But our generation is not unique. From the time Moses led the grumbling

Israelites out of Egypt to Jesus's confrontation with the moneychangers in the temple and unto the present day, evil has always been with us and indeed has been dominant in one form or another. But even in such times, God seeks out people who fear him. Samuel served under a high priest who, through his failures, lost the stewardship of the temple and witnessed the depravity of Eli's sons every day. In his time, messages from God had become so rare he seemed to have abandoned his people. But God spoke to Samuel. For us, the lesson is obvious. We are to live as lights in a dark and perverse generation, even if we see that darkness inside the church sanctuary. Humility, obedience, integrity, and service are still traits that God seeks out. We may not audibly hear God's voice, but he will guide us in his service if we are ready servants.

Israel's Defeat

1 Samuel 4:1b–22

The Big Picture

Ancient peoples, both Israelite and pagan, regarded their religious objects as much more than symbols. Pagans believed that their gods, in some manner, dwelt inside the idols that represented them. The Egyptians, for example, kept the idols of their gods hidden away within their temples, far from the eyes of the common people. On certain holidays, however, the priests would take them out of the temples and load them onto boats with wheels, analogous to our parade floats, and carry the images of the gods on a sacred procession down the main avenue of the city. This would be a time of ecstatic celebration and worship, as the people believed that their gods were literally among them in these images.

The Israelites did not have any idols representing Yahweh, but they did superstitiously invest the ark with the same level of prestige as pagans invested in their idols. Thus, they believed that when the ark came among them, Yahweh himself was especially present and would fight for them. They thought this would make them almost invulnerable in battle (we see the same superstition reflected in the movie *Raiders of the Lost Ark*). The Philistines, as pagans, naturally believed the same thing about idols and sacred objects. When the Philistines defeated the Israelites and captured the ark, it signified one of two things to both the victors and the vanquished: either the gods of the Philistines were stronger than Yahweh, or Yahweh had abandoned his people. They might believe both things simultaneously.

First Samuel 4 corrects the superstition that going into battle with the ark on your side guaranteed victory, and the next chapter will make it clear that Yahweh was stronger than the gods of the Philistines. Also, God did not abandon his people, but he did punish them. Specifically, the entire episode came about because of the godlessness of the priests of Shiloh and in order to fulfill the prophecy of Samuel.

Digging In

The Philistines were part of a group known as the "Sea Peoples" who spread out across the Mediterranean world around 1200 BC. The group that settled near Israel, on the southern coast of Palestine, appears to have been related to the Greeks (although the Greeks as we know them did not enter history until centuries later). Their language, from what little we know of it, is similar to Greek; it was altogether different from the Semitic languages spoken by the Israelites and the Canaanites. It is possible that the Philistines were part of a larger group of Sea Peoples who tried but failed to invade Egypt in about 1180 BC. Repulsed by Pharaoh Ramses III, the people the Bible knows as Philistines established the five cities of Ashdod, Ashkelon, Ekron, Gath, and Gaza, and they immediately made inroads against the Israelites. Samson, one of the last of the judges before Samuel, was the first Israelite leader to do battle against the Philistines.

The first battle mentioned in this text took place near Aphek (1 Sam. 4:1), which was in the plain of Sharon (on the Mediterranean coast) about twenty miles north of Ekron, the Philistines' northernmost city. This implies that they were pushing further into Israelite territory and that the Israelite army went out to check their advance. Defeated in their first encounter, the Israelites thought that they could ensure victory by carrying the ark of the covenant into battle. Apart from the superstition implied here, this violated the laws of the Israelite sanctuary, which indicated that the ark was to be kept in the innermost and most holy portion of the Tent of Meeting (Exod. 26:33). Hophni and Phineas, as the priests of the sanctuary, accompanied the ark (their father Eli was too feeble to go out with it).

Both the Israelites and the Philistines were excited by the arrival of the ark—the former with false confidence and the latter with deep fear. The Philistines knew the stories of how Yahweh had overcome the Egyptians. Ironically, however, that worked to the disadvantage of the Israelites, since the Philistines resolved to fight all the harder (1 Sam. 4:8–9). The outcome was a total rout of Israel. It appears that their battle lines were utterly broken and that the Philistines made it to the rear areas of the Israelite deployment, where high-ranking non-combatants, such as Hophni and Phineas, could be found. They were slain along with much of the Israelite army. When 4:10 says that each Israelite fled "to his tent," it probably does not refer to their camp, which would have been overrun by the enemy. Rather, it means that they ran to their homes (as in 1 Kings 12:16 and 2 Kings 14:12, the word *tent* refers to their homes, even though the people at this time live in houses). In other words, the surviving Israelites scattered to the winds and made their way home.

The Benjamite who brought the news of Israel's defeat was probably fleeing home. Shiloh, where the Tent of Meeting and Eli were, was in the Ephraimite hill country, just north of Benjamin's tribal territory, and the man seemingly passed through it on his way south from the battlefield. He entered Shiloh with his clothes torn and dirt on his head, a sure sign that disaster had struck, and he was expressing his grief (1 Sam. 4:11–12). Eli, no doubt anxious about his sons and the fate of the ark, was awaiting information on the battle. The Benjamite honestly reported the events, not hiding the fact that he fled the battle. As such, Eli had no reason to doubt the validity of the report that Israel had lost, his sons were dead, and the ark was captured. Strikingly, it was the latter news that laid Eli low. For all his faults, Eli genuinely cared about the holiness of the sanctuary, and to him, even the fact that his sons had been struck down by Philistines paled in comparison to the news that the ark was in the hands of the enemy. Unable to bear it, he fell backward, broke his neck, and died (4:16–18).

The account of how the news sent the wife of Phineas into labor and despair illustrates how the people viewed this event as an unmitigated catastrophe. Her indifference to the birth of a son, normally a reason for hope and joy, and her naming of him "Ichabod" (meaning "Where is glory?" or perhaps, "No glory"), show that as far as she was concerned, there would be nothing good in this boy's future. Like Eli, she was especially dismayed by the loss of the ark and could not see how Israel could recover (14:19–22).

Living It Out

Sin and failure among leaders have severe repercussions for those whom they lead. The judgments Samuel pronounced were directed against Eli and his sons, and yet the fulfillment of those judgments brought about the deaths of many Israelites. To be sure, those Israelites were not entirely innocent; we have seen that they were no less superstitious than the pagan Philistines they fought. But this, too, represents a failure of the priests, who were Israel's teachers. The corruption spread from the top down, and so did the punishment. Leaders in our culture, both in the church and the state, bear special judgment for their sins, but the penalties they face are not for them alone. The populace at large, and in the churches, reflect the ideas and actions of their leaders and will share in any judgment that may follow. Those of us who are in leadership positions need to be especially careful, since we bear the greater judgment (James 3:1).

Dagon's Humiliation

1 Samuel 5:1–12

The Big Picture

God speaks to people in a language they can understand. Ancient peoples believed that there were countless gods, and they thought of these gods as having varying degrees of power, of having specific domains (one god might be a war deity, and another deity may enable fertility and childbirth), of having rivalries and alliances, and of fighting among themselves for power and dominance. The Philistines believed that Dagon was their chief deity and that Yahweh was the chief deity of Israel (they did not realize that orthodox Israelite religion was monotheistic, and indeed many Israelites were polytheists). For them, the most pressing issue was, "Whose god is stronger, ours or Israel's?" Initially, no doubt, they thought that Dagon was the stronger god because the Philistines won so many early victories against Israel. But that was only indirect evidence. In the story of this chapter, Yahweh gave them much more direct evidence that Dagon, quite literally, could not stand up to him.

Digging In

Although the Philistines were not indigenous to Canaan and in fact were more closely related to the Greeks, it seems that they quickly adopted much of the local culture and religion. Dagon was an ancient Near Eastern deity worshiped in what is now Syria, Lebanon, and Israel. Almost nothing is known of this god; some say he was a fish god and others a storm god, but this is little more than speculation. The Philistines, when they arrived in the area, probably identified him with one of their gods and worshiped him under his local name. By analogy, the Greeks later identified their gods with various gods of Egypt (for example, they equated the Egyptian god Thoth with the Greek Hermes). The Philistines soon came to regard Dagon as the patron god of their civilization. In the ancient world, it was common for polytheists to treat a single god as the specific god of their people or city (for example, the Babylonians worshiped many gods but regarded Marduk as the patron of their city, and of course Athena was the chief deity of Athens).

In ancient warfare, the victors would plunder the vanquished and set up trophies for their triumph, and there was no greater triumph or plunder than to capture an enemy's gods. It gave a heavenly or spiritual dimension to their victory; their god had, as it were, led the enemy god into captivity. For this reason, they set up the ark in the temple of Dagon. This was not to show reverence for the ark but to show that Dagon ruled over Yahweh. It is not clear why, of the five Philistine cities, the ark was taken to Ashdod. It may be that an Ashdod-based contingent of the Philistine army captured the ark and so claimed it as their own.

The very night after the ark was placed in Dagon's temple, the image of Dagon fell before the ark, like a prostrate worshiper before his lord. They set him back up, but the next night, Dagon had fallen and his head and hands were broken off, making him like an executed prisoner before Yahweh. The significance of this would not have been lost on the priests of Dagon, but it likely would have happened out of sight of the common people, and the news would have only slowly filtered out to the general populace. All the people, however, were afflicted with painful sores. This, together with reports that Dagon had fallen before Yahweh, would have filled the people with panic. They had an angry, powerful deity in the middle of their city!

The affliction, we should note, was not "tumors" in the sense of cancerous growths, but some kind of skin affliction. It could have been an infected swelling of the anus, together with painful swelling in the testicles of the men and vulvas of the women (thus, some translations have "hemorrhoids"). It would have been agonizing, humiliating, and frightening, and the people of Ashdod were in a panic to get this object and the deity associated with it as far from them as possible.

The leaders of the Philistine confederation came together and decided to move the ark to Gath. The text does not say why they chose Gath. It may be that the people of Gath wanted the ark as a trophy and so decided to risk bringing it to their city. On the other hand, Gath was further inland and closer to Israelite territory, and so they many have been thinking that if the plague broke out in Gath, it would be easy to get the ark back to the Israelites (Ashdod was on the coast and further away from Israelite settlements). But Gath suffered the same fate and immediately shipped the ark off to Ekron, another inland Philistine city. The people of Ekron panicked as soon as the ark arrived, and right away they, too, were suffering terribly under the plague. It is important to see that the point here is not that the ark is some super-powerful artifact, as in *Raiders of the Lost Ark*. Rather, it demonstrated the superiority of Yahweh over Dagon and that the Philistines could not capture Yahweh or make the ark into a war trophy.

Living It Out

When the ark was captured, both Eli and his daughter-in-law despaired, thinking that all was lost. Although their sorrow showed true devotion to Israel, their despair showed a lack of faith. God could take care of himself and the ark within the Philistine city. His victory over Dagon and his affliction of the Philistines demonstrated to everyone involved that Yahweh was the true god, the maker of heaven and earth. We, too, are apt to think that setbacks for the church are irreversible calamities, as though the plan of God had been thwarted.

To be sure, defeats can be very bad. When the church falls into apostasy, or when moral failure by church leaders causes scandal, or when Christians become like salt that has lost its savor and so are ineffective, a great deal of evil results. But the work of Christ is not undone, and the will of God is not derailed. If we find ourselves saying, "When the foundations are destroyed, what can the righteous do?" (Ps. 11:3), we must remember that Jesus is still enthroned at the right hand of the Father.

The Ark's Return

1 Samuel 6:1–7:1

The Big Picture

The ark came back to Israel not because the Israelites rescued it but because God forced the Philistines' hand. Its return was a work of God and not of men. Beyond that obvious point, the chapter raises two related issues. First, the Philistines sought and followed the advice of their own pagan priests and diviners, and this advice turned out to be good. They saw definitive proof that the plague upon them had been a work of Yahweh, Israel's God, and they freed themselves from the ark and the suffering that it brought upon them. Why does the narrative go to some length to validate the advice of pagan soothsayers? Second, some people in Israel behaved impiously toward the ark, and they, too, suffered plague. This suggests that the passage is setting up a contrast that could make readers uncomfortable.

Digging In

The ark had been present among the Philistines for seven months when they finally got around to sending it back. This is not surprising.

Transportation and communication were slow at this time, and the Philistines first tried to solve the problems the ark brought with it by moving it among their cities. Even after they had begun to seek the advice of their diviners, it would have taken time for them to get together, come to conclusions about what needed to be done, and communicate it to the various rulers of their cities. Notably, they consulted with their own religious leaders and not those of Israel. The term *priest* could be used for Israelite priests, but the "diviners" were clearly pagan, since Israel was forbidden to make use of such occult practices (Deut. 18:10–14; Ezek. 13:23), and it is reasonable to assume that both the priests and diviners were the Philistines' own. We are not told how these soothsayers came to their conclusions, but we can safely assume it involved taking omens through sacrifices (for example, looking at the liver of a sacrificed animal was a common practice) and perhaps by interpreting dreams and seeking the advice of spirits through séances.

The soothsayers realized that the Philistines had offended Yahweh by taking his sacred ark as a war prize, and that they had to make amends. Otherwise, they would not be acknowledging the power and anger of Yahweh (they would only be getting rid of an object that seemed to bring bad luck). This was an astute observation, as it shows that they knew that their real problem was with God; it was not just that they had a religious object that was taboo.

The soothsayers also told the Philistine rulers that they had to send five sets of offerings since the plague had touched all five of their cities. Also, the offering for each city had to be the same: a golden "tumor" and golden mouse. The objects they offered obviously in some way corresponded to the afflictions that the people had endured. If the tumors were in fact painful swellings in the anus and genital regions, then the offerings would have been golden images of buttocks and genitals. This strikes us as both bizarre and amusing, but there is an analogy from the ancient world. Near the ancient city of Pergamum (in modern Turkey) there was a great temple to Asclepius, the Greek god of healing. People came to the god from throughout the world to be healed, and if they believed he had cured them, they would often leave a model of the body part that had been healed. In the modern museum at this site, you can see many full-sized images of arms, legs, female breasts, and genitalia left behind by devotees.

We can easily understand the five golden "tumors," but why the mice? We should not think of bubonic plague; ancient people did not associate rats with plague (that is a recent discovery), and anyway, the word in question means "mice" and not "rats" (contrary to the NIV). First Samuel 6:5 mentions that mice were destroying the land. This suggests that in addition to the bodily affliction of the tumors, the Philistine fields were being overrun by mice, which were consuming their crops.

The soothsayers also told the Philistines to "give glory to Israel's God." This does not imply that they converted to worshiping Yahweh, but it does mean that they acknowledged that he was a great deity and that they had sinned against him. We see the same expression in Joshua 7:19, where Joshua tells Achan to "give glory to the LORD," meaning that he should confess his guilt. In addition, the soothsayers knew of Israel's history—specifically, they knew that Yahweh had delivered Israel from Egypt but that the suffering of Egypt was prolonged because Pharaoh hardened his heart and refused to relent. They thus wisely told the Philistine rulers not to follow Pharaoh's bad example but to acknowledge that they had sinned against Yahweh.

Cows with full udders obviously would not take off down a road, running away from the calves who could give them relief. As the text tells us, this was a test designed by the soothsayers to determine if the plague had really been a work of Yahweh or if it had just been bad luck. If the cows did the natural thing and stayed near the calves, this would imply that Yahweh was not involved. Also, if the cows did go toward Israel, it would be a sign that Yahweh was willing to accept back the ark and their offering, signaling an end to the event. As we read in the story, the cows pulled the cart toward Israel.

Ancient Beth-shemesh was located in the Shephelah, the low hill country between the high hill country of Judah and the Philistine coastal plain. Beth-shemesh occupied a tiny spit of ground, and you can still visit the site today (but no ancient buildings remain). The modern Israeli city of Beit Shemesh is nearby.

The ark came back and was set up on a great rock. The Bible does not tell us what became of the golden tumors and mice, as though that were a matter of no significance. The people of Beth-shemesh were overjoyed to receive the ark back and celebrated with a sacrifice. But some of them looked inside the ark, an act that was absolutely forbidden (Num. 4:20). God therefore struck down seventy people of the town (the Hebrew oddly says, "and God struck down among the people 70 men [and] 50,000 men," but this is certainly a scribal error because Beth Shemesh could not have had anywhere near that many people). This Israelite town, like the Philistine cities, learned its lesson the hard way. And like the Philistines, they dealt with the problem by sending the ark to another town.

Living It Out

For us, there are at least three clear lessons from this chapter. First, God can take care of his own honor and name. Clerics often want to wage war against those who blaspheme their religion. Muslim clerics, for example, often pronounce death sentences against people whom they perceive to have blasphemed Islam or Mohammed. But the God of Israel did not need armies to intervene and save his ark; he took care of it himself. Second, those who truly blaspheme God commit a great offense and will suffer for it. The Philistines realized this and made a significant offering as restitution, and this was a public admission that they had done wrong and had suffered for it. Third, sometimes Christians can learn something from unbelievers. Perhaps the people of Beth-shemesh thought that because they were Israelites, they would not be touched when they broke the rules and opened the ark. They should have learned from the example and handled the ark with great reverence and care. Instead, they just repeated the earlier mistakes of the Philistines.

Israel's Victory

1 Samuel 7:2–17

The Big Picture

This chapter demonstrates that if Israel was faithful to God, they had no reason to fear the enemies around them. It sets up the later development in the next chapter when the people came to Samuel and demanded a king who would lead them into battle. That is, although they knew from experience that God would fight for them if they shunned idols and kept the covenant, they still wanted a human king to give them security.

Digging In

As we read the text, we might get the impression that after the ark had been at Kiriath-jearim for some twenty years, the people all at once longed to be reconciled to Yahweh, Samuel preached to them, and they repented. But human behavior does not work that way. First Samuel 7:2–4 are a summary statement of two things: First, there was a growing conviction among the Israelites that their relationship with God was broken and needed to be repaired. Second, Samuel was routinely preaching in various locations that the people had to get rid of their idols and foreign gods. The two activities were no doubt reciprocal. As the people became more open to hearing God's Word, Samuel was encouraged to preach more, and as he preached more, people in increasing numbers responded. The process summarized here was probably analogous to events in church history, such as the First Great Awakening in America (roughly 1735–1745), when revival swept through the American colonies. It did not happen all at once, and it did not happen in all places equally, but it did happen.

The culmination of this Israelite great awakening, at the end of the twenty-year period, was when they gathered for an assembly at Mizpah (1 Sam. 7:5). Mizpah was a town in Benjamin, not far from Samuel's home at Ramah, and the region, at times, played an important role in Israel's history (Judg. 20–21; 1 Kings 15:16–22; Jer. 40–41). The passage mentions several activities that constituted their formal reconciliation to Yahweh. First, Samuel prayed for them (1 Sam. 7:5). Second, they ritually poured out water before God (v. 6a). Third, they fasted (v. 6b). Fourth, they made a liturgical confession of their sin as an entire assembly standing before God (v. 6c; the short statement, "We have sinned against the LORD," is probably a summary of a longer confession). The water ritual and the fasting may have taken place while Samuel prayed for them.

The significance of Samuel's prayer is clear: The people were estranged from God, and he interceded on their behalf, just as Moses once interceded for Israel (Exod. 32:11–15). Similarly, the fasting and confession had an obvious purpose; it was meant to show the depth of their remorse over their apostasy. What is not clear is the significance of the water ritual. "Drink offerings" were common in the Old Testament (Lev. 23:18; Num. 29:6, 11, 18–19), but these were libations done with wine, and our text does not call the water ritual a drink offering. While the water ritual no doubt had some symbolic meaning, the passage does not tell us what it was, and we should not speak of what we do not know. At least, however, it added solemnity to the ritual of repentance.

When 1 Samueal 7:6 says, "And Samuel judged the Israelites at Mizpah," it does not mean that he pronounced a verdict on them. It means that they recognized his authority to govern them, as the earlier judges such as Gideon and Jephthah had done. Mizpah was the primary location from which Samuel led the nation.

As with the opening verses, it is easy to misread this passage to suppose that the Israelites first all gathered at Mizpah, then the Philistines heard about it, and then they marched against Mizpah. In fact, the gathering of representatives from all the Israelites would have taken some time, and the Philistines would have become aware of a large amount of traffic converging on Mizpah, and they would have assumed that the Israelites were amassing an army to move against them. They would have mustered their troops and would have begun their march probably around the time that most of the Israelites had gathered there and the ritual of repentance had begun. Thus, the ceremony was interrupted by the fearful news that a Philistine army was on its way. Also, since the Israelites had gathered for a religious pilgrimage, and not for war, they would have been lightly armed and somewhat unnerved by a force coming toward them fully intent on battle. To their credit, they did not scatter to the hills but called on Samuel to keep praying for them (v. 8).

Samuel offered a suckling lamb as a "whole offering" (v. 9), meaning that all of it was burned up and no one ate any of the meat. It was entirely consecrated to God, a symbolic gift indicating that Yahweh was their sovereign. Right in the midst of the sacrifice, the Philistine battle lines formed and began to advance. The Israelites remained where they were in Mizpah, probably under orders from Samuel to stand back and watch God defeat their enemies. Yahweh "thundered" against them, probably meaning that an intense storm suddenly struck, with lightning, high winds, and possibly hail lashing the Philistine troops. The Israelites, hunkered down in the town and not stretched out in a battle line, would have been less exposed to the meteorological onslaught, and at any rate they knew that this was an act of their God. Thus, the Philistines panicked, and the Israelites did not. Only after they broke and fled did the Israelites come out to begin a slaughter of the now scattered and demoralized enemy.

It was common in the ancient world to set up a trophy after a great victory over an enemy. The stone Samuel set up served that purpose, except that it gave glory to God, who actually won the battle, and not to the Israelite army. He called it Ebenezer, which means, "The stone of help" (that is, the stone commemorating the help that Yahweh gave). The Philistines suffered such a severe and unexpected defeat that they did not invade Israel for many years to come, and not at all during Samuel's lifetime. Furthermore, they lost previous territorial gains. They would not enjoy another smashing victory against Israel until the Battle of Mount Gilboa, where they killed both Saul and Jonathan (1 Sam. 31:1–7). The final verses summarize the career of Samuel as Israel's judge and relate back to the comment in 1 Samuel 7:6 that he judged Israel at Mizpah.

Living It Out

This passage gives us two distinct lessons. First, God forgives if we come to him in repentance and faith. Second, we should not forget the grace and help we experience when we turn to God. The Israelites quickly forgot the second lesson. Christians, too, can forget what God has done for them in former days and turn to other helpers in times of trouble.

Day Nine

Israel's Request

1 Samuel 8:1–22

The Big Picture

This passage marks a turning point in Israel's history, when they went from being a nation that, ideally at least, was under God and his laws (a nation that had no human central government whatsoever) to being a nation under an autocrat, the king. The Israelites felt they had good reasons for making this change, but Samuel warned them of the unintended consequences.

Digging In

At the outset, the narrative tells us that Joel and Abijah, the two sons of Samuel, were corrupt and greedy. The claim that Samuel's sons were immoral was accurate. But it was also irrelevant. The crowd used this argument as a cover to ask for a king. It is not as though the nation was faced with only two alternatives: Either accept the rule of Samuel's sons or have a king. They could have deposed the sons without choosing a king. Indeed, the office of judge normally was not hereditary. If there is any blame to be laid at Samuel's feet, it is this: he should have never appointed his sons to serve as judges, both because doing so was contrary to Israel's traditions and because his sons were unworthy of the responsibility.

From its founding, Israel had been without a king and only sporadically under judges, and these judges rarely commanded national assent. Most of them only led their own tribe and people from immediately adjacent areas (even Samuel's sons, who judged far to the south in Beer-sheba, probably exercised little authority in the northern parts of the nation). Also, the Israelites could have looked for other judges, but they did not. From the beginning, therefore, the crowd was playing a dishonest game: Against what they implied, Samuel's sons did not rule all of Israel and there were alternatives to choosing a king, but they presented that as the only option. Not only that, but they moved from having an office that generally was *not* hereditary (and so did not allow unworthy sons to inherit the office) to another office, kingship, that was *always* hereditary and subject to the problem of unworthy heirs.

Samuel was troubled, but not because the people confronted him with the unworthiness of his sons. "When they said, 'Give us a king to judge us,' Samuel considered their demand wrong" (1 Sam. 8:6). He prayed to God, a fact that is meant to signal to the reader that his response was in accord with God's will and not the result of personal peevishness regarding the rebuke concerning his sons. God's response is the key to this chapter: "They have not rejected you; they have rejected me as their king" (v. 7). Israel was supposed to be a true theocracy, a nation ruled by God (not the kind of phony theocracy we see in some medieval states or in modern Iran, in which clerics claim to rule in God's name). Israel had no earthly king because God was supposed to be their king, and the Law (in the Ten Commandments and the rest of the Torah) were God's royal rules by which the nation was to be governed. It is for this reason that when Joshua was ready to die, he named no human successor.

God then commissioned Samuel to give a speech detailing what life under a *human* royal government would be like. Thus, Samuel's speech was a prophetic message, like those given by Isaiah or Jeremiah; we should not second-guess his comments, as though Samuel did not know what he was talking about. Samuel told the people that the king would do the following: He will use their sons as expendable fodder, sending them first into battle (v. 11). He will appoint his personal favorites to positions of power, but will treat other citizens as his slaves, forcing them to donate labor to work in his fields and make weapons for his forces (v. 12). Females too, and not just males, will effectively be his slaves and will do whatever work he appoints them to (v. 13). In addition to the very bodies of the citizens, all the land in the nation will be, in the king's mind, his for the taking, to use for himself or to reward his favorites (v. 14). What land he does not confiscate he will tax, imposing a new tithe on the people beyond what they already paid for the support of the priesthood (v. 15). Summing up, Samuel said that anyone and anything would be the king's for the taking, and the people would all be his slaves (vv. 16–17; the word translated as "servants" in the CSB commonly means "slaves"). In short, the Israelites would revert back to what they were under Pharaoh: the property of a monarch.

It is important to realize that these words came true not only under Israel's worst kings but also under their best kings, such as Solomon. He put such heavy burdens on the people that they were no better than slaves. When they went to his son Rehoboam for relief, the young king declared that he would be even more severe. Having no other recourse, the people rebelled, and the nation was irrevocably divided into two kingdoms (1 Kings 12). But both states were still under monarchies, and the oppression continued. Isaiah, for example, describing how the king of Judah and his favorites confiscated private land for their own use, declared, "Woe to those who add house to house and join field to field until there is no more room and you alone are left in the land" (Isa. 5:8).

The people flatly refused to heed Samuel's warning, and God told him to go ahead and appoint a king. This should be regarded as analogous to God's rules concerning divorce, which God allowed not because it was right but because of the hardness of their hearts (Matt. 19:8).

Living It Out

For believers of every era, the great temptation is to suppose that the nation's salvation is political. The Israelites thought that the instability they saw in their nation could be solved by having a king. In the early centuries of the church, Christians thought that all their problems would be over if the emperor were a Christian. In the medieval church, clerics thought that if they could guide the state, orthodoxy would be enforced, and peace would reign. In all these cases, their solutions came with terrible, unintended consequences. Many Christians today believe that if their political views prevail, righteousness will triumph over evil. We can and should have clear political views and be informed citizens, but we should never baptize our political views or suffer under the illusion that any human institution or policy can bring righteousness to human hearts. Inevitably, our solutions will also suffer unintended consequences, and these may be catastrophic.

Saul's Search

1 Samuel 9:1–13

The Big Picture

When one considers the scope of 1 Samuel, this narrative is quite amazing. The book covers the life and career of Samuel, the entire reign of Saul, and the rise of David. It deals with ongoing wars with the Philistines, the crisis of the fall of Shiloh and the loss of the ark of the Covenant, and most momentously, the establishment of a monarchy in Israel. First Samuel is quite a small book, having to pass over or summarize many momentous events. And still, it devotes a significant amount of space to describing the young Saul's search for his father's donkeys. It could have covered the entire episode in a handful of words, taking the reader directly to Saul's encounter with Samuel in verse 14. Why does it give so much detail about the search for donkeys? The probable reason is that the author wants us to see and appreciate the character of the young Saul. It turns out that he was a fine young man and not at all the monster that emerges in later chapters. Reading this account in the context of the full story of the life of Saul, it tells how a virtuous and promising youth became progressively evil due to a singular sin.

Digging In

As Saul would become Israel's first legitimate king (setting aside the unlawful seizure of power by Abimelech son of Gideon in Judges 9), his story naturally begins with an account of his ancestry. The ancient Israelites considered one's genealogy to be a vital part of one's identity. Saul was from a "prominent" family (1 Sam. 9:1); that is, his family was relatively well off and influential in the community. Verse 2 says that he was a "good" young man (the CSB translates this as "impressive," but it is literally "good"). The verse does not mean that he was merely externally or superficially a fine young man; the narrative of his early life shows that he was genuinely a responsible and humble person. Only later, after years of clinging to power, did his psychological and moral state descend to the degradation we finally see in his behavior. But he was also externally extraordinary, being quite tall at a time when most people were fairly short. We should note, however, that the Bible often makes use of hyperbole (exaggeration for effect). While he probably was a full head taller than many men, we do not need to suppose he was that much taller than every single man in Israel. He was just noticeably tall.

All of that is background information in the account; the actual story begins in verse 3, when Saul and a servant are sent off to find some donkeys belonging to the family that had somehow gotten loose and wandered off. Saul's quest for the donkeys took him on quite a journey. He was from Gibeah, a town in Benjamin a few miles north of Jerusalem. He headed north into the hill country of the tribal territory of Ephraim, making it as far as a region called Shalishah. This was roughly some twelve miles northeast of Gibeah, but this was rugged, hilly terrain, and the actual journey on foot would have been much longer. Finding nothing, they turned west and southwest and went through Shaalim, a region otherwise unknown to us (it is mentioned only in this one place in the Bible). We do not know how long the journey took, but it was at least several days, and by the end of it they were out of provisions (v. 7). Finally, they came back into Benjamite territory and found themselves at Zuph, the region containing Ramah, the home of Samuel.

We already know that Saul was obedient to his father's command and put forth a lot of effort in trying to fulfill his charge, searching long and hard for the beasts. The remainder of the passage tells us more about him. First, he had enough sense to know when to quit and was conscientious of his father's concerns (v. 5). How unlike many young people, who are seemingly indifferent to their parents' worries! Second, he was willing to take counsel from a subordinate. When his servant suggested going to the "man of God" for instructions, he did not dismiss the advice out of hand, but discussed it with him (vv. 6–7). We might be surprised that the servant had to explain to Saul about the existence of Samuel, who was by this time a famous judge and prophet in Israel. But we should remember that Saul was, at this time, still a boy (perhaps sixteen?) and that he probably knew very little of the wider world. Third, we can see in Saul a measure of humility; he did not suppose that because he was from an important family that he could walk up to the prophet and demand an answer. He knew he should come with some kind of a gift to show respect, and that he had nothing of value to give (v. 7). Fourth, we can see that Saul was liked by his subordinate, who volunteered to use his own funds to make a gift (v. 8). The little money the servant had may have been his entire savings; his willingness to offer it to Saul shows real loyalty, and this reflects well on Saul.

Living It Out

We see in the introduction to the life of Saul a worthy son, one who was obedient, well-liked, and respectful. What could account for his eventual descent into madness and murder? In the full account of his life, one episode stands out. Samuel told him unambiguously and with no possibility of retraction that God had rejected him as king. And yet, Saul refused to accept God's verdict. He resolutely clung to power and did all he could to kill God's chosen, David. What Saul should have done is clear: accept God's judgment and work with Samuel and David for a peaceful transfer of power. Refusing to do that, his heart became progressively warped. It was not just the power, but the clinging to power, that corrupted him. For us, the lesson is that we must learn true humility and accept the place that God has chosen for us. If we humble ourselves, God will elevate us. If we cling to what we think is our right, we will destroy ourselves. Power can be very corrupting, especially when we try to hold on to it for too long.

Samuel's Message

1 Samuel 9:14–27

The Big Picture

God legitimately gave Saul the opportunity to become a great king and establish a lasting dynasty. That he did not was Saul's fault, not God's.

Digging In

Having made up their minds to go visit the prophet, Saul and his servant proceeded toward the city gate. The passage then tells us, in an aside, that God had told Samuel on the previous day that the man whom he should anoint as king was about to arrive. When Saul did arrive, God told Samuel that this was the specific man. Why does the text point out these details? They inform the reader that it was by no means by chance that Saul was chosen to be king. Samuel did not see him, think that this was a fine-looking young man, and on impulse anoint him as ruler of Israel. To the contrary, God informed him ahead of time that he had heard the outcry of the people and had selected Saul to save them from the Philistines. This is similar to Exodus 3:7, "Then the LORD said, 'I have observed the misery of my people in Egypt, and have heard them crying out because of their oppressors.'" It suggests that Saul had the opportunity to be a new Moses, a savior of his people. Verse 17 tells us that Samuel did not, through some kind of mix-up, anoint the wrong man. Beyond any dispute, Saul was the man whom God had chosen. No one can claim that Saul's later failure was because the whole thing had been a big mistake or that he should have never been made king in the first place.

Readers who are familiar with the Bible may find this troubling, because Genesis 49:10 appears to say that the chosen ruler of Israel would come from Judah (and, of course, David and then Jesus were from Judah). Why would God choose a Benjamite if prophecy had made it plain that God's king should be from Judah? In fact, to the ancient Israelites, it was not plain. The Hebrew of Genesis 49:10 is quite obscure. Although we can say *in retrospect* that this verse makes Judah the royal tribe, this is more the unveiling of a mystery than it is the fulfillment of a straightforward, unambiguous prophecy. Other Old Testament passages do not speak of Genesis 49:10 as fulfilled in David. Even the passage that declares that David's dynasty would rule forever (2 Sam. 7) never alludes to the Genesis text. Of course, we might say that God in his omniscience chose Saul, knowing he would fail and that David would take his place. But that does not negate the facts that Saul was genuinely God's choice and that he had a legitimate opportunity to establish his dynasty before God. Of course, there are other examples of men who were chosen by God but turned out badly (for example, Samson).

It was a mark of Saul's youth and lack of worldly knowledge that he had no idea that Samuel, by now a renowned judge and prophet in Israel, stood right before him in the city gate. Indeed, Saul at this time had apparently never heard of Samuel. He had to be terribly surprised that "the seer" whom he had just met knew a great deal about him (even that he had been on a quest to find his family's lost donkeys). More than that, the seer made him the honored guest at the sacrifice!

Two aspects of the sacrifice need clarification. First, some may be surprised that Saul and the whole party at the sacrifice were able to join in the meal. But there were several kinds of sacrifices. "Whole offerings" were sacrifices given entirely to God; no one could eat any of the meat. Some sacrifices, such as the "sin offering" and "guilt offering," could be eaten only by the priests and their families (Lev. 6:26; 7:10; 22:10–13). However, other sacrifices, the "peace offering" or "fellowship offering," were essentially communal meals in which a group of people came before God and slaughtered an animal both as an act of worship and as a celebratory feast. These sacrifices were, so to speak, less holy than the others. They did not need to be carried out at Israel's central sanctuary (which was first the Tent of Meeting, and later the temple). Such sacrifices were only a step above the ordinary slaughtering of an animal such as a deer or gazelle (Deut. 12:15), which could be eaten but could not be offered as a sacrifice.

Second, these kinds of communal meal sacrifices did not have to be offered at the central sanctuary, that is, the Tent of Meeting or later, the temple. They could be offered at any location, but traditionally such offerings were made on "high places," such as hilltops or other sites deemed to have special significance. Eventually, however, the "high places" became associated with pagan cults, and their continued existence represented a temptation to apostasy (see, for example, 2 Kings 17:9).

When Samuel and Saul met, Samuel quickly got to the point. First, he assured Saul that the donkeys were found and he need not feel troubled about that matter. Second, he told the young man that he was the hope of Israel: "And who does all Israel desire but you and all your father's family?" Israel was yearning for a king to save them from their enemies, and Saul, as Israel's "desire," was the man to fulfill that hope (1 Sam. 9:20).

We see another example of Saul's humility in verse 21, where he protests that he is not worthy of the favor Samuel has lavished upon him. His claim to be from the least important clan is not necessarily meant literally; it is an exaggerated way of saying, "I really don't deserve all the honors you are heaping upon me." Later in life, Saul would demand to be honored above every other man.

Right away, Samuel began to honor Saul as God's anointed. He saw to it that Saul was served the thigh of the sacrifice, a meaty portion that was also used in rituals for ordaining priests (Exod. 29:27). This communicated to all present that this young man was God's chosen instrument. They finished the meal, stayed the night, and prepared to be on their way.

Living It Out

We must never blame God for our failings. Just as God gave Saul every chance to be a great king, he has given us every chance to be an outstanding and faithful follower of Christ. If we have failed, it is not because God set us up for failure. On the other hand, this text shows us how Samuel submitted to the reality that the people demanded a king, and God authorized him to anoint a king. He did it with good grace, treating Saul as an honored guest. Even when we are disappointed by a decision we believe to be wrong, we should not be peevish.

Saul's Anointing

1 Samuel 10:1–16

The Big Picture

This passage presents the reader with the account of Saul's anointing to be king. It powerfully and clearly demonstrates that Saul's claim to the throne was entirely legitimate. He was anointed by one of Israel's greatest prophets and was empowered by the Spirit of God. No one could claim that he had been an imposter.

Digging In

Although the people demanded a king, and although the success of any king depends upon the consent of those he governs, the actual choice of who would become king was not carried out through a democratic process. Only God, speaking through his prophet, could make that choice. As such, this private ceremony, which was apparently carried out with no one present except for Samuel and Saul, legitimately made Saul the king of Israel. The ceremony was short and to the point and consisted of only three actions. First, Samuel anointed Saul by pouring oil on his head, then he kissed him and pronounced Saul to be the ruler whom God has chosen (1 Sam. 10:1). The anointing with oil was probably symbolic of the Spirit coming upon Saul, empowering him to do the tasks set before him. The kiss probably signified that Samuel willingly and joyfully accepted Saul as Israel's king. The pronouncement was necessary so that there would be no ambiguity about the meaning of the ceremony: Saul was now king.

Samuel then gave Saul a series of predictions concerning what would happen as he journeyed home. They were in Samuel's hometown of Ramah in Benjamin, and Saul would head south toward his hometown of Gibeah. They would almost immediately pass by Rachel's grave, just outside of Ramah. She had died giving birth while traveling south on a road that went from Bethel to Bethlehem in Judah and was buried there (Gen. 35:16–20). This site was important to Benjamites, such as Saul, since Rachel had been giving birth to Benjamin at the time of her death. It was a great honor to Benjamin, and also to Rachel the mother of Benjamin, that Israel's first king came from that tribe. Saul then would meet two men who would pass on the news that the lost donkeys were found and that Saul's father was more worried about his son than the whereabouts of the donkeys (1 Sam. 10:2). This would confirm an earlier prophetic statement by Samuel (1 Sam. 9:20).

Saul would then continue south but then encounter three men heading north to the pilgrimage shrine at Bethel, where Jacob had encountered God (Gen. 28:11–19). The men would give Saul two disks of bread, probably as a simple act of kindness meant to help sustain the young man as he continued on his way (1 Sam. 10:3–4). There is no reason to think they would have recognized him as anyone special. In this context, however, the simple act had an implied significance: the people of Israel were giving Saul provisions, showing that he was their king and that they owed him both honors and physical support. It is as if the three men, without knowing it, were paying taxes.

These predictions, apart from the symbolic meanings already indicated, were meant to convince Saul that God really had chosen him to be king. As Saul saw each prediction fulfilled, he would have understood that the old man who anointed him was not just some old crackpot; he was a true prophet of God.

What most surprises readers, however, is the next prophesy and its fulfillment, that Saul would encounter a group of prophets and would prophesy along with them (vv. 5–12). In Israel at this time, men would come together into small groups and were sometimes called the "sons of the prophets" (1 Kings 20:35; 2 Kings 2:3). We know little about them. They were not the same as Christian monastic orders, although they did form little communities, if only temporarily (2 Kings 4:38–41). Many of them were married (2 Kings 4:1). They were loosely affiliated with the great prophets, and they would have small worship services accompanied by music, waiting to see if God would send his Spirit on one of their members. Saul encountered such a group.

While he was leaving Samuel, God "changed his heart" (1 Sam. 10:9). We do not know precisely what this entailed or how it was manifested, but obviously it was for the good. In some manner, Saul was touched by God. When he encountered the prophetic group, God's Spirit came upon him. The account may be abbreviated. He could have camped with the group so that he was with them when they began their worship service and playing their music in anticipation that someone would prophesy. Or, it may be that he began to prophesy as soon as he met the group without there being any music or preliminary prayer. We also do not know what Saul's "prophesying" consisted of. Did he make coherent prophecies and give the group a word from God, or did he go into some ecstatic trance and do something like speaking in tongues? Whichever it was, the event was unexpected and dramatic. The men there remembered the event after Saul became king, and as people heard how their king had prophesied, they repeated the saying, "Is Saul also among the prophets?"

But someone nearby at the time of the incident said, "And who is their father?" This perhaps implies that some people regarded these prophetic groups with suspicion, wondering to whom they were accountable. In context, however, Saul's prophesying cannot be regarded as a negative event. It was predicted by Samuel in conjunction with Saul's anointing to be king. Therefore, Saul's prophesying was a sign that God was truly with him, empowering him to be king.

When he got home, Saul kept the whole story of his anointing by Samuel a secret, saying only that Samuel told him the donkeys had

been found (vv. 14–19). This tells us that the young Saul was not seeking power. He could have stood up and honestly said, "I am your king!"
But he did not.

Living It Out

It is a dangerous thing to seek authority over others. Christians are
called to humble themselves before God so that he may, in due time,
exalt them. Furthermore, none of us can lead if God has not changed
our heart and empowered us by his Spirit. Saul was off to a great start,
and his life, up to this point, is a role model for us all.

Saul's Elevation to Kingship

1 Samuel 10:17–27

The Big Picture

There are few decisions we make of greater magnitude than choosing a leader, whether that leader be in politics, in a business, in a church, or in a school. We cannot choose leaders precisely as it was done in this chapter, but we can seek God's wisdom and God's will.

Digging In

First Samuel 10:17–19 begin as a typical prophetic speech. Samuel summoned Israel and spoke in God's name: "This is what the LORD, the God of Israel, says." As a premise for his admonition, Samuel reminded the Israelites of how Yahweh had brought them out of Egypt, which is again a standard rhetorical device of the prophets (recollection of the exodus is prominent in prophetic messages). At this point, a prophetic message will begin its complaint against the behavior of the Israelites. Normally, however, that complaint will focus on their idolatry, or it will sometimes speak of their oppression of the poor and widespread immorality. Samuel instead focuses on their demand for a king, seeing that as proof of the apostasy of their stubborn hearts. The act constituted a rejection of God from being king over them.

It is not that having a king was absolutely forbidden to them, as in the manner that worshiping idols was absolutely forbidden. Deuteronomy 17:14–20 does allow them to seek a king. Rightly understood, however, this allowance is a concession; it is certainly not a command, and it permits them to follow the ways of the nations. Imitating the nations is never a good idea, and the allowance to choose a king should be thought of as similar to the allowance for divorce—something God permitted because of the hardness of their hearts. Samuel was well within his rights to criticize Israel for wanting a king (and, of course, he was also giving a word of Yahweh).

Having made his point that their desire for a king was fundamentally wrong, Samuel told them to organize themselves by tribes and clans so that they could have an orderly and proper installation of a king. He then went through the process of choosing a king by lot. Israelite society was organized on the basis of kinship ties, as follows: The nation, called the "Sons of Israel," was divided into the familiar twelve tribes (plus Levi, the thirteenth and clerical tribe). Each tribe was divided into "clans" (these clans or "families" were very extended and would include what we would consider very distant relatives). Each clan was divided into "paternal households." A paternal household would include several generations of nuclear families, including grandparents, their sons and the sons' wives, and the grandchildren. Often, a biblical genealogy can seem incomplete, peculiar, or even seemingly contradictory. This is because many genealogies in the Bible are more concerned with where one fits within the social organization (what tribe or clan or paternal household someone belonged to) than they are with a strict father-to-son genealogical chain.

Using lots for making the selection, Samuel chose one tribe from all the others, Benjamin. And from Benjamin, he then chose one clan, and from that clan, he chose one paternal household, that of Kish. Out of everyone in that paternal household, he chose Saul.

We might wonder why all of this was necessary since God had already told Samuel that Saul was his choice, and Samuel had anointed him. Some people, in fact, argue that 1 Samuel gives us two separate and contradictory accounts of how Saul was chosen to be king (first by anointing and then by lot), and that only one can be right. This, however, is not a compelling conclusion. The process of choosing by lots was a public demonstration of whom God had chosen. Yes, Samuel could have simply gone before the nation and announced, "God has told me that Saul son of Kish is to be king!" The people might well have acquiesced, but they would always harbor doubts about the legitimacy of Saul's ascent to power, and Saul's rule would be compromised from the outset. We read in verse 27 that some people present despised Saul and refused to honor him. How much worse would it have been if he had not been selected by lot? But because they had participated in and observed the process of choosing a man by lots, the majority knew that this had been the will of God. Using lots to determine the will of God was widely accepted at this time (Prov. 16:33). They may have even used the mysterious Urim and Thummim, special stones used for seeking the will of God (Exod. 28:30; Num. 27:21).

We can be confident, moreover, that Samuel did not manipulate the lots. That is, he did not rig the game to make sure that the lot fell on Saul. Instead, the choice of the lots was a confirmation to Samuel and to Saul that the prophetic anointing of Saul to be king had been valid.

We can imagine the scene as the Bible describes it. Saul, who still has no ambition to seize the crown, hears with dismay that his tribe and clan have been chosen. Knowing how this will end and fearing the burden of the office, he runs back to his family's supplies and hides himself. He hears his name called and then hears the confusion and excitement as they search for him. Finally, they find him crouched down among the supplies and bring forward their reluctant ruler. This lack of self-promotion again speaks well of Saul.

When they find Saul, they see that he is a tall, impressive young man. The important point is that he looked like the kind of man they would have wanted as king, but in fact, his looks had nothing to do with why he was chosen. God had chosen him to be king, and the people only discovered after the fact that he looked the part.

For the most part, Saul's reign started well. Men of valor and character were attracted to him and formed the core of his army and his court. Some men, of course, thought nothing of him, perhaps out of jealousy. The young Saul did not retaliate but set about the business of trying to be a good king (1 Sam. 10:27). The later Saul would have cut the critics down where they stood.

Living It Out

We typically choose leaders by consensus (as in a vote) or by appointment from a higher-ranking person (as when a CEO chooses a vice-president in a company). But, recognizing how that leader will impact an entire organization, we as Christians should give this great care. We should pray, evaluate the candidate by biblical norms, and seek counsel. Among churches especially, there are many examples of how the choice of a pastor has enhanced or destroyed the church.

Saul's Heroism

1 Samuel 11:1–15

The Big Picture

Saul's transition from private citizen to effective king was in three steps. First, he was privately anointed by Samuel. Second, he was publicly proclaimed king after a national process of choosing a king by lot. Third, he was forced to act like a king by the crisis at Jabesh-gilead, a city to which Saul and his tribe were closely tied.

Digging In

Ammon was the kingdom located directly across the Jordan River from Israel, in what is now the state of Jordan. For the most part it was a relatively minor power, only infrequently coming up in the biblical narrative in spite of its geographic proximity. Nahash, however, was evidently a highly effective king and military leader. The Israelites were genuinely terrified of him (1 Sam. 12:12). Curiously, Nahash enjoyed very good relations with David (2 Sam. 10:1); this surprises us because in 1 Samuel 11, Nahash is an absolute monster. But it was common in the ancient world for many kings in a dynasty to have the same name, and so the Nahash with whom David had good relations was probably the son of the evil Nahash. If it was one man, he reigned for some four decades, which was very rare and unlikely.

Jabesh-gilead was one of the Israelite cities located east of the Jordan. For that reason, it was isolated from the main body of Israelites west of the Jordan and it occupied territory that Nahash considered to be the rightful property of Ammon. The history of Jabesh-gilead ties it closely to Benjamin, the tribe of Saul, and more specifically to Gibeah, Saul's hometown. Judges 19–21 tells how a Levite and his concubine were trapped by a group of thugs in Gibeah. The men raped and murdered the concubine, and the Levite appealed to the tribes of Israel for justice. The city of Gibeah refused to apprehend and turn over the criminals, and as a result, the rest of Israel went to war against Benjamin. It was a bloody war, and Benjamin's population was drastically reduced. Believing they could not allow a whole tribe to go extinct, the Israelites looked for women who could help repopulate the tribe. They found that Jabesh-gilead had contributed no troops to the war, so they sent a force to attack the city, and they captured four hundred unmarried girls and brought them back to serve as brides to the Benjamite survivors (Judg. 21:12). Presumably, these women bore a lot of children for Benjamin. This implies that a significant number of Benjamites were related to the people of Jabesh-gilead. Since that was where all the trouble started, no place had closer ties to Jabesh-gilead than Gibeah. As such, when Saul heard how Nahash had threatened the people of Jabesh-gilead, he was especially keen to come to their rescue. For all we know, Saul himself may have been a direct descendent of one of the women taken from Jabesh-gilead.

The story begins with Jabesh-gilead, realizing it had no chance of resisting the army of Nahash, seeking to negotiate a settlement. They would declare themselves to be vassals of Nahash if he would spare the city. Nahash responded by asserting that he would accept their surrender only if every man had his right eye gouged out. This was obviously a terrible atrocity, but it had the purpose of humiliating Israel (1 Sam. 11:2). That is, it was meant to send a message to all Israel that Nahash was a powerful and ruthless warrior and that they had better submit to whatever he demanded. This explains the curious feature about verse 3.

Why would Nahash allow Jabesh-gilead seven days to try to rally the Israelites to their defense? From a military perspective, it would have been wiser to capture Jabesh-gilead right away and not give them time to try to find allies, but Nahash was completely confident in his ability to defeat whatever force Israel sent and probably believed, with good reason, that they would send none at all.

Israel, through the time of the judges, had been effectively an anarchic state. They had no central government whatsoever, and they certainly had no national army. When an occasional judge led forces into war, his army usually consisted of men only from his own tribe and vicinity. Of course, Israel's security was supposed to be in God, whom they were to serve as their true king. But the Israelites were routinely apostate and had the worst of both worlds. They had no national army to fight for them, and God was not protecting them. Nahash, knowing that Israel could never put together a large and effective fighting force, happily allowed Jabesh-gilead time to seek the help of the Israelites west of the Jordan. It would only prove his point that they were hopelessly weak.

Saul at this time had only recently become king, and when messengers came to him, he was out plowing his fields (v. 5)! We should remember that Israel at this time had no royal tradition at all, and Saul probably had no idea what he should do as king. And so, he worked his land, as usual. The news about Jabesh-gilead galvanized him into action, however. He cut up his oxen and threatened to slaughter the oxen of any Israelite community that did not send men to join his army and march against Nahash (v. 7). This was something the Israelites had never experienced. Saul was a king, fully exercising his authority, and was threatening retaliation to any Israelites that held back. Very quickly, Saul had an army.

He only had a week to gather his army and get across the river to Jabesh-gilead, and so it is probable that he made the last part of the journey in great haste, as a forced march during the night. He came upon the theater of battle so quickly that Nahash was entirely taken by surprise. The ruse was more effective because the people of Jabesh-gilead feigned acceptance of Nahash's terms. As such, he had no reason to think there would be any battle at all. In the early hours of dawn, Saul assaulted Nahash's camp from three directions, and the Ammonites were utterly routed.

Apart from the salvation of Jabesh-gilead, two important developments came out of this action. First, Saul went from being a king in name only to being a king in fact. He would never go back to living like a private citizen, plowing his own field. He would begin the task of building a national army and administration. Second, Saul discovered what it meant to exercise power. He had threatened violence against his own people should they disobey him. Henceforth, Saul would regard his own word as law. This would begin a pattern of great ruthlessness in governing the people, not only for Saul but for many kings after him.

Living It Out

Political solutions have unintended consequences. The Israelites thought that they absolutely had to have a king. After the process described in 1 Samuel 9–11, they had one. But they also now had a man over them who was ready to commit violence against them and their property should they not obey. Israelite society was changed forever. We should bear this in mind when we are tempted to think that a political action will solve all our problems.

Samuel's Farewell

1 Samuel 12:1–25

The Big Picture

First Samuel 8–12 form a tight unit. Chapter 8 concerns Israel's demand for a king and includes Samuel's solemn warning of all the suffering this will entail. Chapters 9–11 describe the establishment of Saul as king: First, he was anointed as king (chapter 9), then, he was publicly chosen to be king (chapter 10), and finally, he took up the reins of power in a military expedition (chapter 11). Chapter 12 then gives Samuel's farewell address, marking the end of his career as the leader of Israel.

Digging In

Samuel gives what is, in classical literature, known as an *apologia pro vita suá*, a "defense of his conduct of his life." This is a formal statement made by an elderly man at the end of his career justifying the manner in which he carried out the office entrusted to him and answering any charges that some may lay against him. It allows him to end his career in peace and secure his legacy by dealing with any complaints people may have against him. Deuteronomy has many aspects to its message, but it, too, is an *apologia pro vita sua* for Moses, a farewell address in which he asserts that he has faithfully carried out his office. This is why much of Deuteronomy, especially in the early chapters, is taken up with rehashing the sins of Israel. Moses was making the point that their suffering, and especially the forty years in the wilderness, was due to their bad decisions and not because of his leadership.

Samuel thus submitted himself and his sons to the judgment of the populace. No one, of course, could bring a credible charge against Samuel, as he had not treated anyone unjustly or deprived anyone of his rights or property. His sons, however, were another matter, and the text passes over their fate in silence. Presumably, they were at least deposed of their offices. The fact that Samuel began in this way, however, had great significance. The people publicly acknowledged that he had carried out his office faithfully and justly (1 Sam. 12:4–5). This established his moral authority for making his last charge against the Israelites for their turn toward monarchy. Since Saul had just won a great victory, the Israelites may have been feeling pretty good about their decision to crown a king. Samuel meant to tell them, in the presence of Saul, that all was not as good as it now seemed. He invoked the name of Yahweh, who had delivered the nation from Egypt, and called them to hear what their decision to begin a monarchy really meant (vv. 6–7).

Samuel began by retelling the story of Israel from the exodus through the judges period. In our passage, he explicitly mentions how God sent Moses and Aaron to lead them out of Egypt and also the wars against Sisera (Judges 4–5), against the Philistines (Judges 15), and against Moab (Judges 3). He also names four of the judges: Jerubbaal (Gideon), Barak, Jephthah, and himself. As it reads, this is an extremely cursory history of Israel, but it is probably only a brief summation of what Samuel actually said. Large public meetings of this sort could last a very long time in the ancient world; Ezra spent hours reading and explaining the Law to an assembly of the people (Neh. 8:1–2). It is reasonable to assume that Samuel spent a great deal of time working through the history of the judges period. An assembly such as this was how most Israelites learned their "Bible." None of them would have had a written Bible, and many were functionally illiterate.

The main points of Samuel's speech are in 1 Samuel 12 verses 10 and 12. First, verse 10 points out that God always delivered his people when they repented of their idolatry and called on him for help. Second, verse 12 observes that even though they had ample evidence of how God could save his people (he had overcome the power of Pharaoh and warlike peoples such as the Philistines), they were totally unnerved by Nahash the Ammonite and demanded a king. This time, the Israelites had allowed their fear to drive them toward a political and military solution instead of seeking God's help.

Samuel then did something totally unexpected (vv. 16–18). It was around April, the time of the wheat harvest. In Israel, the winter rains nurtured the growing fields of grain, but the spring was warm and dry, the perfect conditions for harvesting the wheat. Heavy rains at this time were rare and would be a disaster, making harvest very difficult and making proper threshing and storage of the grain impossible. And yet, Samuel called for rain, and rain came. This was an act of judgment against the Israelites (threatening them with famine), and it was a sign that Samuel still spoke with prophetic authority. The people understood all of this, and they were terrified (v. 19). Samuel now fully had their attention, and he came to the main point of his message.

Israelite society had fundamentally changed. They had gone from being a loose confederation of tribes to become a monarchy. This would never be reversed. From this point until Israel was destroyed, first by the Assyrians and then by the Babylonians, Israel would know no government except kings. But one thing had not changed at all: Their well-being depended entirely on whether they were faithful to God. If they were, then God would sustain them. If not, no king could save them (vv. 13–15, 20–22).

Samuel's role was reduced to being a teacher and intercessor for the people (vv. 23–25). These are very important roles and not to be dismissed, but he was no longer their leader, the judge chosen by God. This was a signal of a more significant change. Israel was no longer a (true) theocracy, a nation with no earthly king but ruled by God and no capital city but heaven. It was now under hereditary human rule and was only indirectly ruled by God.

Living It Out

No nation today is a true theocracy, under the direct rule of God, and no nation can be. The church is not a political organization; it is a body of people drawn from every nation whose citizenship is in heaven. No government, whether a monarchy or a republic or any other, is God's chosen instrument on Earth. Even as we Christians are involved in politics, we should be wary of political solutions. Every political choice involves allocation of limited resources (pleasing some but angering others), trade-offs (political solutions are almost never purely for the good), and unintended consequences. But this rule remains: "Righteousness exalts a nation, but sin is a disgrace to any people" (Prov. 14:34).

Saul's Unlawful Sacrifice

1 Samuel 13:1–15

The Big Picture

Saul faced a terrible dilemma: he was waiting on a crotchety old man to show up and make a sacrifice, and the longer he waited the worse his military situation became. But that old man was Samuel, and he spoke for God. If Saul wanted God's help, he would need to show patience and faith.

Digging In

First Samuel 13:1, in the Hebrew, is quite astonishing. It literally says, "Saul was one year old when he became king, and he reigned for two years over Israel." This is obviously not plausible. Some interpreters have tried to explain the verse as it stands as a kind of metaphor for Saul's inexperience, but this is not persuasive. It is far more likely to be a scribal error. This means that somewhere along the line, a scribe miscopied the text, and his mistake was then perpetuated when other scribes copied his manuscript. Scribal errors are most likely to occur with proper names or with numbers. This text involves errors with numbers. When such an error occurs, translators often emend the text; that is, they suggest a corrected reading. The CSB has done this, and so has translated the verse, "Saul was thirty years old when he became king, and he reigned forty-two years over Israel." However, this is conjectural. We do not know how old Saul actually was when he became king (for myself, I believe he was closer to twenty when he became king).

The episode that follows took place well into Saul's reign. We know this because his son Jonathan was old enough to command troops and was a skilled warrior. Saul at this time had a standing army of three thousand men. Of these, two thousand were with him preparing for a campaign against the Philistines near Michmash, and one thousand were garrisoned with Jonathan at Gibeah, Saul's home and capital city (Michmash was located a few miles to the north). The other Israelites had been sent home and were, in effect, the reserves. But it was actually Jonathan who initiated hostilities. He struck the Philistine garrison at Geba, located between Gibeah and Michmash. We are told nothing about the battle, but apparently Jonathan routed the Philistine defenders.

The Philistines, we should note, maintained garrisons in Israel, which they considered to be their vassal in spite of Philistine setbacks during the time of Samuel. From these garrisons, the Philistines would have kept an eye on the Israelites and collected tribute. The forces of Israel under Saul and Jonathan were ready to begin the task of driving out the Philistines for good, and this meant striking out against their garrisons. An attack on one of these garrisons, moreover, would be a declaration of war.

When the Philistines got word that their outpost at Geba had been attacked, they mobilized for war. Saul, knowing that the die was cast, did the same (when he "blew the ram's horn, 1 Sam. 13:3, he was calling up the reserves). The full army came together at Gilgal (located east of Michmash and near the Jordan River), which served as a national place of assembly (1 Sam. 10–11). The Philistine army headed toward Michmash, where Saul had been previously. This was an important pass in the hill country and thus vital for controlling the theater of operations.

As the Philistines approached with their infantry and chariots, the local Israelites were terrified. The Philistines were better trained and equipped and were almost what one could call professional soldiers. The Israelites were essentially peasants with makeshift weapons; they were a civilian militia with no real training or unit cohesion. Furthermore, chariots were at this time weapons meant to create panic in opposing infantry. They would charge into battle, often with a driver and an archer in the chariot. They were actually of little value against a well-trained infantry, who would form up in a line behind their shields. Against a loosely organized group of light infantry lacking military discipline, they were extremely useful. The chariots would scatter the light troops, allowing their own infantry to march in and cut down any remaining opposition. The Israelites whom the Philistines encountered while on the march, therefore, would not stand to fight at all. They hid themselves in caves and bushes, and some ran all the way to the east side of the Jordan, to the territories of Gad and Gilead.

Saul, meanwhile, was stuck back at Gilgal waiting for Samuel to show up and perform the obligatory sacrifice before the army could set out. Day after day, Samuel did not appear. Saul had the best troops under his command. His troops included militia but also included the regular army that was experienced and more capable of standing up to a Philistine charge. And yet, they could do nothing until Samuel arrived.

For Saul, this was nothing short of a catastrophe. The Israelite people were scattering, and no doubt the homes that lay in the path of the Philistine army were being plundered and burned. Men in his own army were losing heart and beginning to melt away. The narrative makes this vividly clear: We are *meant* to have sympathy for Saul's predicament and see things as he saw them. After seven days, Saul finally gave up on Samuel and offered the sacrifices himself. And of course, as soon as the sacrifices were done, Samuel showed up!

Saul justified his actions on the grounds that he had to seek God's favor with a sacrifice, but Samuel would have none of it. He told Saul that what he did was foolish and that as a result of his actions, his dynasty would not endure (1 Sam. 13:13). He did not, at this time, declare that Saul was no longer the rightful king, but he did assert that God had already chosen a different man to replace him. There would be no enduring Saulide dynasty.

We might well wonder why the punishment on Saul was so severe, especially after the narrative had gone out of its way to tell us how desperate things had become. Any reader can sympathize with Saul's distress over Samuel's tardiness and understand why Saul did as he did. We might well assert that the main point was simply Saul's disobedience to God, and certainly there is truth in that (v. 13). Both David and Solomon arguably did worse things, however; Solomon actually sponsored shrines to pagan gods (1 Kings 11:4–6).

The reason Saul's sin was so great was that, if left unpunished, it would create a terrible precedent for the monarchy. Specifically, it asserted that the king could usurp the proper role of the priests and Levites. That is, the king would have become Israel's high priest, just as the pharaoh was the high priest in Egypt. This would have destroyed the institution of the Levitical priesthood that God had set up through Moses. It was a precedent that could not stand.

Living It Out

We all at times feel that our situation is so desperate that we are entitled to break God's rules. This is never a good idea. Our experiences are not unique, and we cannot change the rules because our plight or our emotions strongly demand that we go in a different direction. God and Saul's army would have still defeated the Philistines, no matter how long it took for Samuel to arrive. Saul, however, thought it all depended on him and forgot to rely on God.

Israel's Weakness

1 Samuel 13:16–23

The Big Picture

In this passage, nothing actually happens. That is, there are no battles or betrayals. Instead, it is an account of what life was like for the Israelites as they lived under the oppression of the Philistines. It also explains something that before now the book had only hinted at, that the Philistines had an enormous technical advantage over Israel and thus also had military supremacy. The Bible, in Judges, had frequently spoken of how this or that people "oppressed" the Israelites, but in this text, we get a specific portrayal of what that actually meant.

Digging In

There were two types of empires in the ancient world. Most of us, when we think of ancient times, with its battles and wars and imperial expansion, think of the Roman Empire as it existed in New Testament times and later. This was an empire in which the central imperial power (Rome) directly administered its empire through governors and other provincial officers appointed from the capital. It was, in many respects, as if the empire were a single nation governed directly by a single king. Although there might be local kings and ruling families for a time in the Roman Empire, these tended to die out or be replaced as the control of a local territory came to be more and more under the direct administrative control of Rome. Eventually, all the lands of the Empire were effectively annexed to the central government. For example, Judea and Galilee were under both local kings (such as the Herods) and governors appointed by Rome (such as Pontius Pilate) during the lifetime of Jesus, but within a few decades, the Herods were gone and the territory was directly under Roman control. Modern counterparts to Rome would be the United States and Canada, which simply annexed territories as they expanded westward and became huge, centrally governed states.

But there was also a second kind of empire, and this was much more common earlier in history. In this model, the conquering state and the conquered state remained separate entities, each with its own local government. For example, around 1350 BC, Egypt had an empire that included all of Canaan, but the Canaanites maintained their local governments; as a national entity, Egypt remained inside its borders. The Egyptians maintained garrisons in Canaan, however, and the Canaanite states were vassals and required to provide tribute to Egypt. Similarly, Judah in the late seventh century BC had its own king but was a vassal of Babylon. Although local areas such as Judah were semi-autonomous, the Babylonians, like any such empire, could be very harsh. When Judah stopped paying tribute, the Babylonians destroyed Jerusalem and took the people captive, not annexing Judah but eliminating it altogether.

This was the kind of empire the Philistines had over Israel. They did not directly administer the territories of Israel, but they maintained garrisons in Israelite lands to be sure that the Israelite population and leaders remained subservient. Samuel's earlier victory over Philistia had evidently checked their expansion and, to some degree, weakened their hold, but Philistine domination was still much in evidence in their outposts and garrisons within Israelite territory.

Apart from having garrisons among the subdued people, this kind of empire also looked for another kind of "choke-point" to enable it to maintain control. Some kind of economic domination or technical superiority could serve that purpose. The British Empire, for example, did not annex places such as India, but it did maintain control through a combination of economic domination and superior technology, especially military technology. The Philistines did precisely the same thing, as they had technical superiority in the field of metal working. Early on, they were probably more innovative than the Israelites, so that the Philistines had iron weapons well before their enemies. During the early part of the Iron Age (1200–1000 BC), very few people had iron tools or weapons; most still used bronze. Philistines, with their iron weapons, could defeat Israelites wielding bronze. As their domination grew, the Philistines maintained their supremacy by force, using violence to prevent any Israelite blacksmith from opening shop.

This monopoly in blacksmithing served the Philistines in two ways. First, it allowed them to drain Israel economically, as Israelites had to pay Philistines for any metalwork they wanted done. Second, it allowed the Philistines to maintain their military superiority. Philistine blacksmiths would make plowshares and pruning hooks for the Israelites, but no swords or spears. Again, this kind of mercantilist empire has counterparts in the early modern period, in the empires of Spain and England. When 1 Samuel 13:22 says, "So on the day of battle not a sword or spear could be found in the hand of any of the troops who were with Saul," it may be to some extent exaggerating for effect, but the point was valid. The Israelite peasants, holding a variety of farm tools and obsolete weapons in the face of the "modern" Philistine regiments, would have been a pathetic and woe-begotten excuse for an army.

The Bible is quite specific in describing the Philistine stranglehold over Israel, even giving the prices they charged for work involving plowshares, axes, and other agricultural tools (v. 21). Unfortunately, it is all but impossible to put those prices into their equivalents for twenty-first-century America (we are not even sure what the Hebrew words in this text for the prices mean), but we can be sure that for the Israelite peasant, the prices were exorbitant. And the money all flowed one way, from Israel to Philistia (striving for this kind of economic domination, what we would call a "trade imbalance," is the essence of mercantilism).

As the Israelites faced the Philistines, they were a backward and depleted people, lacking real weapons and with little national cohesion. From this point, first under Saul and Jonathan and then under David, they would grow to become a great empire in their own right. They would reach the high point of wealth, military power, technology, and cultural sophistication under Solomon. This was a testimony to the tenacity of these men but also of the mercy of God toward his people.

Living It Out

Deuteronomy 28 describes all the woes that would befall Israel for apostasy from God and his covenant. Among these woes, verse 33 says, "A people you don't know will eat your land's produce and everything you have labored for. You will only be oppressed and crushed continually." Our passage for today showed how this prophecy played itself out in the life of Israel. It is a warning to us that when any people become self-indulgent, immoral, and apostate, tangible and terrible results will follow. People will scoff at such warnings, but the suffering that comes of disobedience will be intense.

Jonathan's Heroism

1 Samuel 14:1–23a

The Big Picture

This passage tells how Jonathan, through his heroism and faith, began the process of driving out the Philistines. It also sets up Jonathan as a parallel to David—two young men with great courage and confidence in God. These traits would be the basis for their strong friendship.

Digging In

After his stinging rebuke from Samuel, Saul and the men around him became disheartened. Those who had gathered to Saul and Gilgal scattered, and Saul retreated with a small force of about six hundred men to his hometown of Gibeah (1 Sam. 12:15). The Philistine army, having accomplished its objectives, evidently returned home. They had thoroughly demoralized the Israelites, forced them to flee and to hide, and had checked any plans Saul may have had to gather and train a significant army. They did, however, leave behind a garrison at Michmash, a pass that controlled communications in the central hill country of Israel (13:23). This would, they probably supposed, prevent Saul from making a second attempt at forming an army. We may wonder why they did not immediately pursue Saul and seek to kill him and annihilate his small force, but the terrain was very rugged, and a protracted campaign of trying to root out a small force held little hope for success. Later, Saul would find out just how hard such a campaign could be when he tried to catch David and his band of followers. Also, with the troops wanting to get back to their farms as quickly as possible, military campaigns at this time tended to be very brief affairs. Thus, some of the Philistine troops may have returned home.

Jonathan, however, having provoked one war, now set about provoking another. Verse 1 tells us that he did not tell his father, Saul. This implies that Saul would have prevented him from going out, and not just out of concern for Jonathan's safety. Saul had seen how badly things turned out in the last war with the Philistines, and he was probably not wanting another one. He remained in Gibeah with his six hundred men (1 Sam. 14:2), probably glad to have escaped the last war with his head still on his shoulders.

The text also gives us two additional pieces of information. First, Saul's "court" was held at a pomegranate tree on the outskirts of Gibeah, in a place called Migron (v. 2). Sometimes, in the Bible, a tree becomes well-known as a significant location (for example, the oak of Mamre of Gen. 13:18). But for Saul to have held court under a tree tells us how primitive the Israelite monarchy was at this time. He certainly did not have a royal palace! Second, Ahijah was wearing "the ephod" in his court. An ephod was a garment somewhat like a vest that was worn by priests. Thus, Ahijah was serving as the resident priest in Saul's court. It may be that, after the previous episode involving the sacrifice, Saul decided that he had to have a priest with him at all times. Ahijah was the nephew of Ichabod and great-grandson of Eli. We recall that many years earlier, after the Philistines defeated the Israelites and took the ark, Eli died and his daughter-in-law went into labor, giving birth to Ichabod (1 Sam. 4:21). Samuel had declared that, because of the ungodliness of Eli's sons, his descendants would lose the high priesthood (1 Sam. 3:14). We cannot say that it was wrong for Saul to use Ahijah as a priest, but Saul's dynasty is already beginning to look doomed to failure, and it is curious that a doomed royal line was served by a doomed priestly line.

To get up to the Philistine garrison at Michmash, Jonathan had to climb between two columns of rock, which the local people called Bozez and Seneh (v. 14). This detail simply adds color to the narrative, making it more vivid. It has no theological importance. At any rate, this approach was quite difficult, but Jonathan and his armor-bearer made it. Jonathan called the Philistines "uncircumcised" (v. 6). Circumcision was, of course, the mark of the covenant for the Israelites, but it also, in their minds, marked them as clean, civilized men in contrast to the unhygienic uncircumcised. Jonathan was in effect calling the Philistines barbarians. Jonathan also came up with an impromptu plan to seek a sign from God, saying that if the Philistines called them up, that would be a sign that God would give them the victory (vv. 8–9).

In the event, Jonathan and his armor-bearer killed about twenty men, which may have annihilated the garrison there. This was a great victory, and the Bible attributes it to God's help and Jonathan's bravery, but there may have been another element at play as well. Combat at this time focused on great champions. We see the same thing in the Homeric battles of the *Iliad*, and later, of course, David would fight as a champion against Goliath. An honor code may have required the Philistines to fight Jonathan one at a time instead of as a mass of twenty against two. Thus, Jonathan may have won twenty successive victories in single combat—no small feat! In addition, Philistine pride could have been involved, since they viewed the Israelites as cowards (v. 11).

In combat by champions, a defeat can have tremendous psychological impact, and the Philistines, alarmed at the news of such a humiliating defeat, quickly fell into panic and confusion. Their fear was intensified by a series of local earthquakes (v. 15). Saul's scouts and runners began to report back that the Philistines were in disarray, and he quickly determined that Jonathan had gone out and stirred things up (vv. 16–17). Saul realized it was time to strike, and he considered taking the ark of the covenant into battle with them but changed his mind (vv. 18–19). He may have recalled that the last time Israel took the ark into battle, things went badly for them (1 Sam. 4).

The narrative of verses 20–23a covers a somewhat extended period of time. Saul initially took his small force out from Gibeah and struck down a nearby Philistine unit, and this in turn encouraged other Israelites to rise up against the enemy. Even Israelites who had collaborated with the foe turned against them. Furthermore, Philistine uncertainty about what to do led to internal squabbles and bloodshed within their own ranks. Soon, Philistine garrisons all over the country were falling. Jonathan had been the spark, and God used him to create a great conflagration.

Living It Out

The situation could hardly have been more hopeless for Israel when Jonathan and his armor-bearer set out for the Michmash Pass, but his courage and confidence in God were the basis for a mighty work of salvation. God does not need large numbers or military power, but he does need someone to have faith and to act upon it. As Jonathan said, "Nothing can keep the LORD from saving, whether by many or by few" (v. 6).

Saul's Foolish Vow

1 Samuel 14:23b–46

The Big Picture

We sometimes get the impression that all of the bad people in the Bible are irreligious and that all their sin grows from the fact that they either have no belief in God or are apostate. But this is often not the case. Often in the Bible as in the modern church, people do foolish and evil things because they have a genuine but ill-informed, superstitious, or perverted belief in God. Remember that Jesus was not taken for crucifixion by pagans or atheists, but by Jews who firmly believed that they were upholding orthodoxy and the true faith. In this text, we read how Saul's real but confused faith led him to do something very foolish, with severe repercussions for Israel.

Digging In

The battle was moving to Beth-aven, a little north of Michmash, when Saul decided to make a vow: "The man who eats food before evening, before I have taken vengeance on my enemies is cursed" (1 Sam. 14:24). Saul did this from a sincere belief that by making such a vow he

73

would ensure that God was on his side; he would ensure that his men fought all the harder and would show himself to be a heroic leader. The taking of a grand, impressive sounding vow was not rare among military men, and it is always a kind of posturing and posing. The wise soldier knows that events are never fully in control, and one can never know that things will work out in such a way that he can keep his vow.

Saul's vow was not unprecedented. The most foolish vow in the Bible was that of Jephthah, who vowed that he would sacrifice the first thing that came out of his house to God. He probably assumed that this would be one of his cattle, because Israelite homes often had what we would regard as a barn on the first floor. But in fact, his daughter came out first. Jephthah kept his vow by sacrificing her (Judg. 11:30–40; some people think that he did not sacrifice her but put her into something like a convent, but this is not plausible). Jephthah's superstitious religion forced him to keep his vow; he would have been more righteous had he broken his vow, not murdered his daughter, and confessed that he had vowed foolishly. Another vow, quite similar to Saul's, was when a group of Jews vowed that they would eat nothing until they had murdered the apostle Paul (Acts 23:14). When the Roman tribune heard of this, he took Paul out of danger and foiled the plot. One can imagine that those men soon became very hungry! The making of a vow is dangerous, since it is a promise to God. For this reason, Ecclesiastes 5:5 says, "Better that you do not vow than that you vow and not fulfill it."

Needless to say, Saul's vow had a terrible impact on his forces. They were in hot pursuit of the Philistines, but having had nothing to eat, they soon became exhausted and weak. Even so, their fear kept them from taking any of the honey that they saw in the forest. Jonathan, however, did not know anything about the oath, as he was not present in the assembly in which it was proclaimed. When he saw the honey, he reached out with his staff to retrieve a bit of it (he apparently did not use his hands in order to avoid getting stung) and ate some. Being of high sugar content, it quickly gave him energy. The Hebrew expression in 1 Samuel 14:29 for "I have renewed energy" is literally, "My eyes shine."

A soldier then told Jonathan about Saul's vow, but even that soldier knew that it was foolish, for he said, "Your father made the troops solemnly swear, 'The man who eats food today is cursed,' and the troops are exhausted" (v. 28). Jonathan, who was a man of deep faith, immediately knew that Saul had done something that was both militarily and theologically wrong; He had weakened his own forces, and he had tried to impress God and coerce him into fighting for Israel.

In the course of events, the troops actually ended up doing something truly wrong. When they finally got to and defeated a group of Philistines, in their desperation for food they slaughtered some animals and ate the meat without properly draining the blood. This act, consuming blood, violated the first dietary restriction, and the only *universal* dietary restriction, in the Bible (Gen. 9:4). This was far worse than a taste of honey.

Saul finally got the men under control and set up a stone for slaughtering animals where the blood could be properly drained before the meat was roasted, and so he put an end to what, in Israelite culture, was a true abomination. We should note that this kind of sacrifice did not require someone like Samuel to carry it out. It was primarily a meal, and as long as the animal was not unclean (like pork) and the blood was properly drained, there were no other religious restrictions. They also had a priest, apparently Ahijah, present for the sacrifices (1 Sam. 14:36).

At this point, with the troops fed and reenergized, Saul was ready to continue the attack on the Philistines. The priest, however, encouraged him to seek God's guidance using the Urim and Thummim stones to cast lots. He agreed, but no answer came from God. Saul surmised that someone had broken the vow he had made and announced he would kill the miscreant (v. 39). When they cast lots to find the culprit, it of course turned out to be Jonathan. We should note that God held Saul to his vow in that he would not answer Saul's inquiry until the matter of the eaten honey had been resolved. This does not mean that God wanted Jonathan put to death. He was, in fact, innocent; he could not keep a vow he knew nothing about. But Saul, like Jephthah, was ready to go through with it and kill Jonathan. His troops, however, dismayed at such a miscarriage of justice, prevented that. Discouraged about how what should have been a great victory turned into a day of fiasco, however, the army broke off its pursuit of the Philistines.

The immediate result was that Israel achieved a much smaller victory than they could have had. The long-term results are harder to be sure of. Jonathan did not live to become king after his father, but that is probably not because of the broken vow. Samuel had already told Saul that he would have no dynasty to follow him (1 Sam. 13:14). However, the incident may have haunted Saul in the years to come. As he became more distraught over the prospect of losing the crown to David, he became progressively unbalanced, even insane. He may have been tormented by his vow and the thought that Jonathan should have died.

Living It Out

We Christians can be tempted to think that our faith makes us morally superior and that anything we do in the name of God will turn out well. That, however, is just not the case; Christians can do very foolish things, even when they think they are acting as a step of faith. Our actions must be guided by the discernment that grows out of daily study of the Bible and the maturity that comes from interaction with believers who have demonstrated wisdom in the conduct of their lives. Experience, sound teaching, good examples, and a humble spirit will keep us from the folly people commit in God's name. When we fail to do this, we have no right to expect God to bail us out just because we were sincere about our bad decisions.

Saul's Reign in Summary

1 Samuel 14:47–52

The Big Picture

Saul took on a very tough job. We have seen that the Israel he ruled had no tradition of a central government, no standing army, and in many respects, was an impoverished, backward, disorganized, and scarcely united nation. On every side, enemies pressed down upon him. This man whom we first met as a humble youth wandering the hills in search of his father's donkeys spent nearly his entire life at war. The Israel that David inherited was not a loose confederation of independently thinking tribes; it was a powerful, united nation. David had Saul to thank for that, and he never lost his respect for the strength and achievements of Israel's first king.

Digging In

First Samuel 14:47–48 and verse 52 are a summary of the major achievements of Saul's reign, and verses 49–51 list principal members of his family and the names of his leading officers. In the narratives of the kings of Israel, this is a sign that the account of the life of this king is drawing to a close. Only one more incident will be entirely focused on Saul's reign, the account of his sin in the war against Amalek (1 Samuel 15). After that, although Saul will continue to be king through the rest of 1 Samuel, the real focus of the story will be David. Indeed, after the anointing of David in chapter 16, it is an open question whether Saul, in the eyes of God and of Samuel, was still the legitimate king.

Verse 47 does not list the wars of Saul in chronological order. It mentions Moab first, but we know that his first great campaign was against King Nahash of Ammon (chapter 11). The list is a summary, making no mention of how many times or under what circumstances he fought a given enemy. Moab was located east of the Dead Sea and had fought Israel ever since the time of Moses. Ammon was located east of the Jordan River and at times viciously attacked Israel, as in Nahash's plans for Jabesh-gilead. Edom was located south of the Dead Sea, in the low territory called the Arabah and was Israel's perpetual enemy. Zobah was an Aramean kingdom located north of the Beqaa Valley of modern Lebanon; Saul's wars with Zobah would foreshadow many more wars between Israel and the Arameans of Damascus. The Philistines were located on the Mediterranean coast southwest of Israel. A glance at a map is sufficient to confirm the claim that Saul fought Israel's enemies "in every direction" (1 Sam. 14:47). Saul's Israel was surrounded by hostile forces. This is important not only because it is testimony to Saul's tenacity in the face of great odds; it shows that he was truly a national king, looking out for all the tribes and clans from north to south and east to west. Saul's physical courage and military prowess were unmatched: "Wherever he turned, he caused havoc, and he fought bravely" (vv. 47–48). The last enemy that verse 48 mentions is the Amalekites, a nomadic people from the Arabian desert. This war would be the occasion of his moral downfall, but this verse mentions only that Saul was victorious and brought deliverance to the Israelites whom the Amalekites would plunder. This passage is plainly saying that whatever his faults, Saul's achievements deserve recognition.

The account of Saul's family is brief because he did not establish a lasting dynasty; there is little need for a lengthy genealogy or list of descendants. Nevertheless, the names of his wife and children are given in honor of Saul. The list may not be complete: Abinadab (1 Sam. 31:2) and Ish-bosheth (2 Sam. 2:8) are not named. It may be, however, that Ishvi is a variant name for both men. Saul's daughter Michal would play a significant role in David's life. It is perhaps surprising to us, with our tradition of seeking to avoid nepotism in office, that Saul's cousin Abner was his chief military commander. But remember that Saul's capital was his hometown; this was a kingdom built from scratch. Saul naturally staffed his high offices with people he knew and trusted. As far as we can tell from the rest of the narrative, Abner was highly capable and served Saul loyally. David, too, made his close relative, Joab, the commander of his army.

First Samueal 14:52 states, "whenever Saul noticed any strong or valiant man, he enlisted him." This tells us two things. First, Saul was an efficient king and commander, determined to build up Israel's military. Second, the prophecy of Samuel was coming to pass: "He will take your sons and put them to his use in his chariots, on his horses, or running in front of his chariots" (1 Sam. 8:11). Saul truly took a collection of politically free, if disorderly, tribes and turned them into a monarchy. Henceforth, the youth of Israel would serve the state.

Living It Out

William Shakespeare famously has Marc Antony say at Caesar's funeral oration, "The evil that men do lives after them; / The good is oft interred with their bones" (*Julius Caesar*, act iii, scene 2). This is true for the powerful and famous generally, and it is especially true for those in politics and the church. A president such as Warren G. Harding is principally remembered for the scandals that entangled members of his administration, although he was arguably a very fine steward of the government and economy. A pastor or Christian leader may do a tremendous amount of good, and do it out of deep convictions and faith, and yet, if he should get caught up in a sexual scandal, that is the only thing he will be remembered for. Billy Graham, in his great wisdom, went to extraordinary lengths to avoid even the hint of any kind of scandal or sexual entrapment associated with his ministry.

He knew that no matter how faithfully he preached the gospel or how many successful crusades he led, such a thing would be the destruction of it all. The Bible does not begrudge the achievements and heroism of Saul. In certain areas, he failed so badly that he lost the kingdom, but this does not undo the good he did. We should not hide the failures of others, but we should not think that their sins and failures were all that they were. A mature soul can appreciate the good in others even if it also has to mourn the evil.

Saul's Repudiation

1 Samuel 15:1–35

The Big Picture

When Saul wrongfully offered a sacrifice in Samuel's place, God told him that his dynasty would not endure (1 Sam. 13:14). Conceivably, Samuel (and God) could recognized Saul as the rightful king till the end of his days, with the understanding that his dynasty would collapse soon after his death and another would take his place. In this passage, Saul himself loses his right to rule the kingdom. In a real sense, Saul's reign is from this point on no longer legitimate.

Digging In

In 1 Samuel 15:1, Samuel recalls that he anointed Saul to be king at God's command. This implies that Saul was still the legitimate king. Furthermore, it makes the command Samuel is about to give Saul all the more solemn: God chose Saul for a purpose, and now Saul must fulfill that purpose. The issue at hand is the Amalekite problem. These were nomadic tribesmen from northern Arabia. They were closely associated with the Midianites, but whereas the Midianites were often peaceful and well-disposed to Israel (remember that Moses's father-in-law, Jethro, was Midianite; Exodus 18), the Amalekites were hostile in the extreme. They were a kind of band of desert raiders who raided unsuspecting villages to slaughter and pillage, carrying off any survivors to the slave markets. Israel also had a special grievance against Amalek; they had treacherously attacked Israel while it was sojourning in the wilderness toward Mount Sinai, and for this reason, Moses had declared that there would be perpetual hostilities between Israel and Amalek (Exod. 17:8–16; see also Num. 24:20, 24). This is the incident referred to in verse 2 of our reading today. Amalek had continued to be a problem, raiding Israelite villages and terrorizing the people (for example, Judg. 3:13). The Amalekites of our passage were plundering villages all across the southern part of Israel ("from Havilah all the way to Shur," 1 Sam. 15:7).

Samuel's commission to Saul contains a very severe element: "Now go and attack the Amalekites and completely destroy everything they have. Do not spare them. Kill men and women, infants and nursing babies, oxen and sheep, camels and donkeys" (1 Sam. 15:3). This is called the *herem*, a Hebrew word traditionally translated as "ban." It was the most extreme form of warfare, requiring the complete annihilation of an enemy people and even the destruction of all their property and livestock. In the conquest narrative, the *herem* was applied to the city of Jericho.

Naturally, readers are troubled by this. We should note, however, that the *herem* was quite rarely applied. All the many wars against Ammon, Moab, Edom, the Philistines, and other peoples never involved the *herem*. Also, readers who feel moved to pity the Amalekites know none of the backstory—the bloodshed, terror, and enslavement that they routinely carried out (see v. 33). There was also a theological and psychological element to the *herem*. In applying it, Israel effectively said, "We are not simply engaging in a tit-for-tat with you, attacking and plundering you as you have attacked and plundered us. We declare before God that you are unfit to remain in this world. For this reason, we will not only exterminate your people; we will destroy your livestock to make clear that we are not looking for plunder. We are turning you and all you have over to God for judgment."

Saul, the vigorous warrior that he was, carried out a thorough campaign and routed the Amalekites, finally capturing their main body and their leader, Agag. Saul first warned the Kenites to stay out of the theater of battle (v. 6). Of all the Midianite peoples, the Kenites were the most well-disposed to Israel, and he is not criticized for this act. Saul and his men, however, kept the best of the livestock for themselves. This was an act of greed, not of pity. Saul allowed Agag to live, perhaps as a sign of chivalrous obligation to a fellow king. But of all the Amalekites, this was the worst man to spare. He was the one man who could have gone back to their Arabian homeland and put together a new Amalekite fighting force. Saul's disobedience was in every respect inexcusable.

Samuel, as part of his rebuke to Saul, put Agag to death (v. 33). We should note that there are no grounds for thinking that Agag was a forefather of Haman the "Agagite" of the book of Esther. The similarity of names is coincidental, and Haman was almost certainly a Persian and not an Amalekite. Any family Agag had would have presumably died in the *herem*.

The central point of Samuel's rebuke is in verse 26, "Because you rejected the word of the LORD, the LORD has rejected you from being king over Israel." Saul, in a panic, clung to Samuel and begged him not to publicly humiliate him. This was a futile gesture; when Samuel returned with him (v. 31), it did little more than save face for Saul. When Samuel's garment tore (v. 27), it implied that there was nothing Saul could do to retain the crown. It was over.

We may ask what Saul should have done, and the answer is simple: accept God's verdict. He could have offered to resign immediately in favor of whomever God should choose or, if it seemed best, to remain in a caretaker role until the new king was sufficiently trained to take power. Instead, he fought desperately to keep the crown, trying to kill David and even threatening the life of Samuel (1 Sam. 16:2). The young man who once said he was unworthy to be king (1 Sam. 9:21) now refused to release his hold on power and prestige. Had Saul been willing to step down, he would have avoided the murder, madness, and ignominy that marked his later reign.

Living It Out

The most beautiful and moving words of this chapter are those of Samuel to Saul: "Does the LORD take pleasure in burnt offerings and sacrifices as much as in obeying the LORD? Look: to obey is better than sacrifice, to pay attention is better than the fat of rams. For rebellion is like the sin of divination, and defiance is like wickedness and idolatry" (1 Sam. 15:22–23). Christians who know the context may find this language to be less appealing, since in this case the obedience demanded was the slaughter of an entire people. However, when we consider more fully the background and significance of this command, we cannot so easily dismiss it as something Saul was right to disobey. And of course, God is God, and just as he gave life, he has the right to take it. The words of Samuel remain true; disobedience of a direct command of God is a heinous sin, and no amount of religious behavior, church attendance, or tithing can cover for it. Either God is our Lord, or he is not.

As a secondary matter, we should observe that sometimes we can love a job too much. There comes a time to let it go, either because we know we are not qualified, or because we cannot support the policies of the institution, or simply because it is time to leave. Hanging on to a position too long can ruin a person's good legacy.

David's Anointing

1 Samuel 16:1–13

The Big Picture

In this section, Samuel anoints David to be the next king. In the course of events of Israelite history, this was truly momentous. In the narrative, however, it was a quiet episode in an out-of-the-way place involving a boy whom no one, not even his own father, expected to amount to anything.

Digging In

Verse 1 tells us that Yahweh had to rouse Samuel and compel him to go anoint Saul's successor; Samuel was so overcome with grief over Saul's failure that he had become immobilized. This rebuke has two important implications for the reader. First, the picture we have seen of Samuel repeatedly rebuking Saul is misleading. Those were only a couple of incidents drawn from years in which Samuel quietly and apparently happily accepted Saul's conduct of his office. Samuel did not despise Saul, he had no desire to micromanage Saul's administration of his office, and he certainly did not want to remove Saul from power. He genuinely loved Saul and wanted him to succeed, rebuking him only when necessary and at God's command. Saul did not lose the crown because of meddling or antagonism on Samuel's part. Second, Samuel did not relish the role of playing kingmaker. He did not anoint David because he was looking for someone he could control. He went to anoint a new king reluctantly and from a divine compulsion.

From what we can tell in the narrative, Jesse, the father of David, was not an impoverished peasant. He had a large family and maintained a significant amount of livestock. He was a direct descendant, and apparently the grandson, of Boaz (Ruth 4:21–22). Ruth portrays Boaz as an important figure in Bethlehem, at least what we would call upper-middle class. When told to go to "Jesse of Bethlehem," Samuel may have already known the name.

Samuel, to our astonishment, asserted that Saul would kill him if he anointed a successor to replace him (1 Sam. 16:2). Although we have not seen it thus far in the narrative, Saul was apparently beginning to show the tyranny and desperation that characterized his later years. Next, to our even greater astonishment, Yahweh told Samuel to engage in what we can only term a deception. Although his real purpose was to anoint the man who will take Saul's place, he was to tell everyone that he had simply come to make a sacrifice. We have a similar dilemma in Exodus 1:17–21, in which the midwives who "feared God" lied to Pharaoh about how Hebrew babies escaped being put to death, and God in turn showed favor to the midwives.

Interpreters have different ways of dealing with this dilemma, but in my view, the best solution is that moral reasoning is hierarchical, so that some rules are weightier than others (see Matt. 23:23). In particular, the act of allowing a corrupt government to kill an innocent person outweighs the act of deceiving that government, so that in such a case deceiving the government is no sin. Thus, for example, a person who lies to SS officers of the Nazi regime, telling them that there are no Jews hiding in that basement and so saving the people who actually are in the basement, is being righteous, not evil. In the same manner, Samuel had no moral obligation to allow Saul to kill him for following God's command and anointing a new king.

Samuel thus set out for Bethlehem. We do not know why the people there were frightened at his arrival (1 Sam. 15:4), but it is probably that any arrival of a great prophet could portend bad news. It is perhaps analogous to the anxiety people feel when the CEO of a large corporation suddenly shows up in a section of lower ranking office workers, where he is generally never seen. They all ask, "Why is he here?" But Samuel reassured the people of Bethlehem that he had no bad news to deliver and put them, more or less, at ease.

The locals, including the family of Jesse, had to be consecrated. That is, they had to undergo a process of ritual cleansing before they would be allowed to partake of the sacrificial meal. Although we don't know precisely how this was done, Samuel had some direct role in consecrating each person at the sacrifice (v. 5). This allowed him to look at each of Jesse's sons individually. On looking at the eldest, Eliab, he was so impressed by the young man's demeanor and appearance that he thought that this had to be the one God had chosen (v. 6). God, however, told him that this was not the case. Jesse's next sons, Abinadab and Shammah, were similarly rejected, as were all seven of David's brothers present there. We should note that Eliab, who had so impressed Samuel, turned out to be a churlish, overbearing bully (1 Sam. 17:28).

God memorably told Samuel, "Do not look at his appearance or his stature because I have rejected him. Humans do not see what the LORD sees, for humans see what is visible, but the LORD sees the heart" (1 Sam. 16:7). We are all inclined to accept or reject people based on superficial and even quirky reasons. We don't like the color of a person's hair, or the way she pronounces a word, or his short stature. In motion pictures, heroes are rarely portrayed by homely actors. We should not go to the other extreme and claim that external appearances mean nothing. An employer might with good reason refuse to hire someone who comes to an interview slovenly dressed or otherwise indifferent to his appearance. Still, it is the heart—a person's character, integrity, and attitude toward others—that really matters. God can see the heart directly and is not deceived by superficial efforts to impress or by seeming deficiencies in appearance.

At last, Jesse brought his youngest son David to the gathering, and Samuel anointed him (vv. 11–13). It turned out that David was a fine-looking boy (v. 12), but that neither qualified him nor disqualified him for the job. David said nothing at all in this episode; unlike Saul, he did not protest his unworthiness (1 Sam. 9:21). If we can venture a guess, he was probably bewildered by the whole experience. Also, Samuel did not make a series of predictions to validate his actions, as he did with Saul (1 Sam. 10:1–8). David's situation, however, was noteworthy in one respect; he was the younger brother, and thus he was thought to be least likely to succeed. But he was chosen by God to lead his people. In this, he follows the pattern of other younger brothers, Jacob and Joseph.

Living It Out

We make no choices as important as the choosing of people. We choose who will be our intimate friends, who we will marry, who we will hire for a job, who will be our governor, and so on and so forth. All of these have enormous impacts, for good or ill, on our lives. By comparison, choosing which car to buy is trivial. None of us has direct insight into the hearts of other people, but we can and should seek God's guidance and learn discernment.

David's Lyre

1 Samuel 16:14–23

The Big Picture

This passage has some strange things in it: a spirit that distresses a king, music that soothes a tormented mind, and a remarkable series of events that brought David of Bethlehem to the court of King Saul. It is, above all, a tale of God's providence.

Digging In

As the Spirit of God came upon David (1 Sam. 16:13), it left Saul (v. 14). This is something we do not fully understand, but in some manner God's Spirit gave his anointed courage and wisdom, enabling him to lead Israel. Its presence or absence must have in some way been apparent to people since Saul's servants could tell when an evil spirit was tormenting him. This experience, the loss of God's Spirit and the arrival of an evil spirit, should have made Saul eager to lay down his crown. But it did not.

The evil spirit sent from God to torment Saul is also something of a mystery. Saul was not demon possessed; or at least, he was not possessed as we normally think of it. The spirit would come and go (v. 23), and a possession appears to be permanent until the demon is permanently removed, as in the exorcisms performed by Jesus. People try to explain the evil spirit upon Saul in several ways. Some say that Saul was mentally ill—perhaps bipolar—and that an "evil spirit" was simply how ancient people diagnosed and explained his affliction. In this interpretation, Saul was not really afflicted by a spirit; he was sick. Some might say that the spirit was "real" but not personal. In other words, God sent some kind of affliction upon Saul, but that affliction was more of a strong influence than a personal being, as when we might say, "A gloomy spirit pervades this place." Exodus 35:21 (NRSV) speaks of people who had a "willing spirit," which was an inner disposition and not a heavenly being (many other passages are similar; see Ezek. 13:3; Prov. 29:11). Against these options, however, is the view that the spirit was a demonic being sent to torment Saul. There was a "lying spirit" in 1 Kings 22:21–22, and he was clearly personal, since he spoke directly to God. A complication is that, at least initially, the playing of music could lift Saul from his depression and drive the spirit from him (v. 23). It is not clear to us how playing music could chase away a demon. Finally (although this gets us into fairly deep water!), there is one other point to observe: When the spirit is a personal being (a demon), it is presented in the masculine gender, as in 1 Kings 22:21. When the spirit is a prevailing attitude or disposition, it is feminine (as in Exod. 35:21). The "spirit" in 1 Samuel 16 is feminine, suggesting it is more of a disposition.

On the other hand, I am not sure we can or should choose between the three options. Saul was clearly mentally ill, and his condition worsened as he aged and grew more frustrated with his inability to overcome David. Second, his affliction in some respect did concern his own inner disposition as it was influenced by God as an act of judgment. Third, we are in no position to deny that a demonic spirit was involved in Saul's demise.

It so happens that as I am writing these chapters, I am also reading a major biography of Adolf Hitler. It is astonishing how this ne'er-do-well, an obviously strange and warped man with no achievements and of limited ability, could rise to absolute power over one of the world's most advanced people and lead them into a maelstrom of death and destruction. I would suggest this: First, a kind of mental illness— fueled by dismay over defeat in the First World War and above all by pervasive anti-Semitism—gripped the German people. Second, a hysterical, frenetic, but *impersonal* spirit pervaded masses of Germans, especially at the great Nazi rallies. Third, the great evil of the Third Reich was also Satanic in origin. My point is that the three options need not be mutually exclusive.

To return to our story: Saul's associates, recognizing that he needed help, suggested music therapy. They believed that a skillful lyre player could sooth his tormented mind and enable him to have some peace. It appears, although we cannot be sure, that this was several years after Samuel had anointed David. In the previous story, David was evidently so young that he was thought unfit to be among the men at a sacrificial meal with Samuel. In this text, he is "a valiant man, a warrior, eloquent, handsome, and the LORD is with him" (v. 18). The latter statement means that to all appearances, David was doing well in life and was blessed by God; the speaker was not claiming to know precisely what God thought of David. But it is clear that the David of verse 18 is already in the early years of manhood; he had already been to war. Saul, who was obviously unaware that Samuel had anointed David as his successor, summoned David.

The fact that David was known by someone at Saul's court suggests that his family was not obscure. Also, since Jesse wanted his son to make as good an impression as possible, he sent along bread, wine, and a goat as a gift for the king. These were not the gifts of a great aristocrat, but they do imply that Jesse was no impoverished peasant.

David's arrival at court was a great success. His music did indeed soothe Saul, and the king was so impressed with him that he made the young man his armor-bearer. This was a position of very high honor, as it indicated that the king trusted David with his life. An unreliable or cowardly armor-bearer would, in time of battle, surely get the king killed.

Living It Out

"We know that all things work together for the good of those who love God, who are called according to his purpose" (Rom. 8:28). If there was ever a man who was called for God's purpose, it was David. Saul's affliction meant that he had to have music therapy, and by chance, as it were, someone at court knew that David was a talented musician. Because of this, David was brought into Saul's inner circle and was making a name for himself before anyone thought of making him the next king. The narrator wants us to discern the hand of God behind all of this. If we belong to Christ, we should have some sense of the calling he has for us, and we should be aware of how he has providentially led us in the way we should go. Our faith is not just that God watches out for us, but that he prepares the way for us even when we know nothing of it.

Goliath's Challenge

1 Samuel 17:1–11

The Big Picture

Goliath stood before Israel as an apparently unbeatable enemy. He was, to all appearances, the quintessential warrior. But if the Israelites had remembered that God was with them, they could have overcome their fear and thought clearly about how to face him. Goliath was most definitely beatable. Instead, as they listened to his challenges and taunts, Goliath seemed to get bigger every day.

Digging In

We are suddenly transported to a battlefield, with the Philistines lined up against the Israelites. The passage does not tell us when this event occurred. It does, however, tell us the location of the battle, at Ephes-dammim and in the Valley of Elah. This was in the Shephelah, the low hill country on the west side of Judah. The Philistines lived in the Mediterranean coastal plain, and the Shephelah was contested territory between the high hill country of central Judah and the coastal Philistine enclave. Both armies naturally occupied high ground for their camps, and the valley in between the two forces was the natural place for them to engage one another.

But the armies did not simply march down and start fighting. Instead, the Philistines sent out their champion, Goliath, to challenge the Israelites and demand that they send out a champion to fight him. As we have already discussed, combat by champion was practiced at this time, and this kind of warfare was something of a military ideal in early Greek societies (remember that the Philistines appear to have been related to the Greeks and to have migrated from the periphery of the Greek world). In the *Iliad* of Homer, we see how combat almost always focuses on great champions such as Achilles, Ajax, and Hector. Thus, it seems that the Philistines decided to try to achieve a cheap victory by sending out a seemingly unbeatable champion. The Israelites were familiar with the idea of combat by champion, and honor demanded that they not simply ignore the challenge. Either by losing to Goliath or by not sending a champion at all, the Israelites might have to surrender without ever having engaged the Philistine army in combat.

Goliath is said to have been six cubits and a span tall, or in our terms, a staggering nine feet, nine inches. However, some ancient manuscripts have a different number: four cubits and a span, or about six feet and nine inches. We should remember that in ancient texts, names and numbers are the most likely words to be miscopied. Even to us, a man of six feet and nine inches would be extraordinarily tall, and to the ancient Israelites, who were relatively short, he would have seemed enormous. More than that, Goliath was extremely strong, as he wore very heavy armor. He was something of a one-man tank. He also had a pike (not a spear for throwing but a pike for skewering an enemy) that was like a "weaver's beam" (1 Sam. 17:7). This appears to mean that it was made from a thick, heavy shaft of wood. There is, however, something here that the modern reader can easily miss.

In the ancient world, there were two basic varieties of infantry. The first, heavy infantry, wore plate armor and carried large shields and long pikes. The idea was to keep the soldier as well-protected as possible and to enable him to engage an enemy at some distance with the long pike. Only after the enemy had gotten inside the reach of his pike would he drop the pike and use a sword. At this time, however, heavy infantry tactics were not well developed. Within a few centuries after David's fight with Goliath, armies would learn that heavy infantry soldiers were most effective in massed formation, with the men lined up shoulder-to-shoulder in long rows with their shields overlapping and forming a solid "shield wall." As long as they maintained cohesion, they were almost invulnerable, and they could march across a battlefield rolling over less organized opposition. However, a heavy infantryman by himself was far more vulnerable. He was so burdened with armor and equipment that he could do little more than march straight ahead, and he could be cut down from the side or back. But since heavy infantry tactics were as of yet not well-developed or understood, the Philistines simply loaded up Goliath with as much armor as he could carry and sent him out to do single combat.

The second type was light infantry or skirmisher. These men wore little or no armor and fought individually or in very loose formations. They typically carried a projectile weapon (either a slingshot or a bow and arrows), and perhaps a small sword or lightweight wicker shield. They valued fleetness of foot and maneuverability above armor and brute strength, and they sought to kill or disable the enemy from a distance. Against a disciplined, tightly arrayed formation of heavy infantry, light infantry had no chance, but in one-to-one combat, the light infantryman actually had some distinct advantages. As Goliath came out to make his challenge, his shield-bearer walked out in front of him, but when actual combat began, he would hand the shield to Goliath and withdraw, because he had to face the other champion in single combat. This would further burden the Philistine giant. Even Goliath's great pike, as thick as a weaver's beam, would be of limited utility in this kind of combat. Such pikes were especially useful against a man charging on horseback or against another company of heavy infantry, but not so much against a fleet-footed skirmisher.

But when the Israelites looked across the field at Goliath, all they saw was a gigantic warrior with lots of weapons and an impenetrable armor. No one noticed that he had made himself virtually immobile. In their unthinking fear, the Israelites could only conceive of standing before Goliath face-to-face, the two combatants slamming weapons into each other. In this type of fight, Goliath was indeed bound to win.

Aware of their fear, Goliath subjected them to daily taunting: "I defy the ranks of Israel today. Send me a man so we can fight each other!" (1 Sam. 17:10). Forgetting that they were the people of God, Saul and his men allowed Goliath's size, armor, and weapons to paralyze their minds. "When Saul and all Israel heard these words from the Philistine, they lost their courage and were terrified" (v. 11).

Living It Out

While it may seem trivial to turn Goliath into a metaphor for the troubles we face (We all at some point have to face a giant!), he does provide a real lesson for us. Big problems and bitter hostility from others are a reality of life. They can seem unconquerable, and if we give in to fear, our "giants" will only get bigger and bigger. Faith in God means that we know that God loves us and can deliver us from any trouble, but it means more than that. It frees us from fear and allows us to face our troubles more realistically and even creatively. God not only saves by miraculous intervention; he saves also by giving us the confidence and clarity to face the challenges of life.

David's Victory

1 Samuel 17:12–58

The Big Picture

When Israel faced Goliath, everyone in the army looked at it as a military problem. Who could beat this man? David looked at it as an affront to God. Would the God of Israel be able to defeat a really big man? For David, the answer was obvious, and he was determined to show everyone on the field of battle, both Israelite and Philistine, that Israel's God was not to be trifled with.

Digging In

We face an obvious difficulty in comparing this passage to 1 Samuel 16. There, David is a young man—already an accomplished warrior—and he joins Saul's court as a lyre-player and so thoroughly impresses Saul that he becomes the king's armor-bearer. This position implies a high level of trust in David, and it would have required the two men to spend a great deal of time together. Saul would have come to know David very well. Furthermore, David became a permanent resident of the court (1 Sam. 16:22). But here in chapter 17, David is still the shepherd of the family sheep. He is not Saul's armor-bearer, and Saul does not know him at all (vv. 55–58). His only military duty is to shuttle food to his three older brothers, who are on active duty in the army.

Various solutions to this problem have been proposed (and the issue is more complex than I have described here), but in my view the best solution is that the account is not fully chronological but is in part thematic in design (that is, incidents are grouped together because they are similar in content and not precisely according to when they took place). It is possible, therefore, that David fought Goliath (chapter 17) before he played the lyre for Saul (chapter 16).

A popular misconception is that David was a mere boy of thirteen or fourteen years when he fought Goliath. This is primarily because of verses 38–39, in which David says he can't move while wearing the armor of Saul and takes it off. People assume that as an undeveloped adolescent, his thin arms and legs could not handle the weight of the armor, but this is not the case. We have already seen the distinction between the heavy infantryman and the skirmisher. David plainly intended to fight as the latter; the sling was his weapon of choice. To fight in this manner, he needed to be able to move freely and avoid Goliath's efforts to engage him directly. Wearing armor would have significantly *decreased* his chances of victory, but that was because of his style of combat and not because his muscles were weak and undeveloped. Also, in 1 Samuel 17:33, Saul called David a "youth." But like its English counterpart, the Hebrew word for "youth" can be used for a young man and not just an adolescent. Although relatively young, perhaps eighteen or twenty years of age, David was a grown man at the time of the battle.

On the other hand, this was clearly David's first experience of mortal combat with an enemy soldier. If he had been in battle before, he would have surely mentioned that, but he spoke only of his experience fighting wild animals (vv. 36–37). And yet, the man who recommended David to be Saul's musician in 1 Samuel 16:18 described him as a "warrior." It is most likely, therefore, that the fight with Goliath took place when David was a young man and still taking care of the sheep, before he permanently entered Saul's service. After that, his brilliant victory over the Philistine giant coupled with his musical skill caused Saul to make him a permanent member of the royal court. But because David's military prowess dominates the following chapters (see 18:1–9), the editor chose to put the Goliath episode in its present position, after the matter of the lyre playing.

With this understanding, the story itself is quite straightforward. David arrived at camp bringing provisions for his three eldest brothers and saw the commotion as Goliath issued his daily challenge. He then heard specific details from an anonymous soldier, who told him that anyone who could defeat the Philistine would marry Saul's daughter and be wealthy for life (1 Sam. 17:25). David was incensed at Goliath's blasphemy and chagrined that no Israelite soldier had the courage to take up his challenge (v. 26). Eliab, David's eldest brother, probably embarrassed by his own cowardice, tried to cover it by showing contempt for the young man whose main job was still to tend sheep: "Why did you come down here? Who did you leave those few sheep with in the wilderness? I know your arrogance and your evil heart—you came down to see the battle!" (v. 28). David, apparently used to this kind of treatment, turned from his brothers and continued to speak to other soldiers and eventually found himself standing before the king. David was able to convince the king to let him fight as Israel's champion. This was perhaps not a very hard choice since the army was now deeply demoralized and no one else was going to step up. The Israelites would soon be in total disgrace if something wasn't done.

As we have seen, David chose to fight as a skirmisher and shunned the king's armor. He chose five good stones for his sling and, with no other weapon but his familiar staff, went out to face his opponent. Combat at this time was fought at close quarters, and the combatants regularly sought to intimidate one another prior to the fight with insults. Goliath did this, cursing David in the name of his gods and promising to leave his dead body to the wild animals (vv. 43–44). David responded in a much more serious tone, using words that were meant as much for his fellow Israelites as they were for Goliath. David's true strength was not in human weapons but in God, and Goliath had defied God. David's unexpected victory would show the world that Israel belonged to God. "The battle is the LORD's. He will hand you over to us" (v. 47).

Goliath then walked toward David (walking was the best pace he could maintain), while David ran toward Goliath (even though he had no intention of taking on Goliath face-to-face, the slingshot still had a limited range). David's shot struck Goliath's unprotected forehead and at the very least stunned him badly, if it did not kill him outright. But that did not matter; David decapitated Goliath with the giant's own sword. Seeing their champion suddenly struck dead, the Philistines panicked and were easily routed by the exultant Israelites (v. 52).

If David had told Saul his name earlier, the king had quickly forgotten it. Now, however, he was profoundly impressed and determined to learn what he could about the giant-killer (vv. 55–58). This agrees with 14:52, which says that Saul was always on the lookout for competent warriors to enlist.

Living It Out

David was not the greatest warrior Israel had ever seen. Indeed, there were many slingers in Saul's own tribe of Benjamin who could have gone out to face Goliath (Judg. 20:15–16). Unlike them, however, David had an unshakable faith in God and a deep certainty that God would honor whoever honored God. Skills and training are good, but to stand in the face of the great crises of life, we need faith in God more than we need great ability.

David's Rise in the Court

1 Samuel 18:1–30

The Big Picture

Bringing a successful newcomer into an organization can easily prompt one of two reactions. Some will be thrilled to have a competent and energetic addition to the team, knowing that his success will enhance the success of all. Others, however, will be jealous, seeing him as a threat to their position and prestige. In this passage, David, the slayer of Goliath, enters Saul's entourage and enjoys a meteoric rise, having multiple achievements and winning enormous adulation. In response, one prominent member of the team will do all he can to help David, but another will try to get him killed.

Digging In

The narrative of this chapter is in three movements. First, David became amazingly successful in war and won the adulation of everybody (1 Sam. 18:1–5). Second, Saul became insanely jealous of David and tried to kill him (vv. 6–16). Third, Saul tried to use the promise of a marriage to get David killed (vv. 17–30).

This chapter covers a considerable span of time. David was Saul's armor-bearer for a while (16:21), but he eventually became a military officer in command of his own unit (18:5). It obviously took some time for David to accumulate so many victories that women began to sing of how he had slain "tens of thousands" (v. 7). There is some tension between 1 Samuel 16:22, which indicates that David became a permanent member of the court as a result of his musical work, and 18:2, which implies that Saul first kept David with him right after the fight with Goliath. It may be that Saul retained David in camp for some time after the Goliath battle but then sent him home, and only later, after he had received permission from Jesse to retain him (16:22), established him in the royal court.

And David was successful! All the people came to love him. Jonathan was so impressed that he made a private covenant with David. This would be renewed on later occasions (1 Sam. 20:16; 23:18). This friendship would prove to be one of the most stable and enduring relationships of David's life; it was cut short only by Jonathan's death in battle (1 Sam. 31:2). Jonathan's reaction to David speaks well of his character and distinguishes him from his father, Saul. Jonathan was himself a great military hero and could have looked at David as his father did, as a rival in the chase for glory, but Jonathan had a generous soul. He happily praised the accomplishments of a fellow Israelite even if those deeds outshined his own.

It is not clear precisely what meaning Jonathan intended to convey in giving David his own robe, cloak, sword, bow, and belt. Some interpreters believe that he was declaring that David should be the next king; that is, they think Jonathan was announcing his abdication from the position of crown prince! But we have no evidence that the act had such enormous symbolic significance, and it seems astonishing that Jonathan should have surmised at the very beginning that David was destined to take the throne. At most, Jonathan's gift may have signified that he and David were wearing the same colors and were, so to speak, on the same team. A much more reasonable interpretation, however, is that David was very poor. As the eighth son in his family, he had no prospects of getting any money from that source. Apart from the fact that Jesse had eight sons to provide for, the ancient Israelites had no notion of dividing property equally among their offspring. The older sons received far more than the younger sons. When David showed up at the camp, his tunic, staff, lyre, and sling probably comprised the entirety of his worldly possessions. He had neither the clothing necessary for abiding in Saul's court nor the weapons necessary for fighting alongside Saul's troops. Clothing and weapons at this time were extremely expensive, because making them was labor-intensive. Jonathan, as a member of the royal house, had plenty. His sharing with David was more an act of generosity than it was a political statement.

As time went by, David won more victories, and from Saul's perspective, this was a problem. He was now determined to hold the crown and pass it on to his son, but he knew that Samuel had prophesied that his family would lose the throne. As such, he viewed the rise of David with alarm (1 Sam. 18:8). At the same time, some of his reactions appear to have been also personal and emotional. His response to the little song that became popular among the girls of Israel, "Saul has killed his thousands, but David his tens of thousands" (v. 7), suggests that Saul could not bear for someone else to get more praise than himself.

This began his process of mental deterioration, punctuated by episodes in which Saul abruptly grabbed a javelin and tried to skewer David within the royal court. We can hardly imagine what the atmosphere of the room was like. Did Saul rage and make threats after the javelin missed its target? Or did he laugh it off, saying that he was just trying to test David's reflexes? We do not know, although it must have been apparent to all that the king was coming undone.

Eventually, Saul collected his wits enough to realize that an outright murder of David would badly undermine his position as king, and he sought a new strategy. His first thought was to give David his eldest daughter Merab in marriage, supposing that this would show he harbored no ill feelings toward the young man. He could then send him out on dangerous military missions until David finally was killed, and he could do so while avoiding suspicion that he had set it all up. This was of course terribly evil, but we should remember that David used a similar strategy to get Uriah the Hittite killed (2 Sam. 11:14–17). In this case, however, the plan failed. David was the impoverished eighth son of his father and he could not afford the requisite bride-price, and he was of low social status. To take her under these conditions would be a dishonor to both Merab and David. Thus, he politely refused, and Saul married her off to another man.

Sometime later, Saul learned that Michal, his second daughter, had fallen in love with David. He devised a new strategy: He would accept one hundred Philistine "foreskins" (in reality, penises) as the bride-price. This was a brutal age, and a severed penis was proof that the original owner had been killed. For the Israelites, it was grimly appropriate, since they despised the Philistines for being uncircumcised. Saul, then, was asking David to show his valor by killing one hundred Philistines, thinking that the quest would surely be the death of David. To his chagrin, David killed two hundred Philistines, and Saul had no choice but to accept the man he now regarded as a dangerous rival as his son-in-law.

Living It Out

The jealousy of Saul is in stark contrast to the generosity of Jonathan. The father became progressively evil and insane; the son lived with honor and integrity. Jealousy, this text tells us, destroys the human soul.

David's Escape

1 Samuel 19:1–24

The Big Picture

This passage shows us three tests of character within a single family. Saul was tested for whether he could keep his word and not give into jealousy over David's success. Jonathan's loyalty to David was tested: Would he do what was right or betray his friend without just cause? Michal, David's wife, was also tested: Would she be loyal to her husband or to her father, knowing as she did that the former was innocent, and the latter had become violently unstable?

Digging In

First Samuel 19 begins quite dramatically with Saul abandoning all subterfuge and ordering his attendants, including his son Jonathan, to outright murder David. Once again, we do not know how much time elapsed between David's marriage to Michal and the beginning of this narrative. Jonathan, of course, had no intention of allowing David to be killed and he sought a diplomatic solution. He first told David to get away and hide so that he could have time to try to reason with Saul.

Verse 3 is somewhat difficult to understand: If Jonathan brought Saul to the field where David was hiding so that David could overhear the conversation, why would Jonathan need to tell David what Saul said? It may be that Jonathan only wanted David to see that he was pleading with Saul for David's life. That is, David may not have been able to hear everything, but he could observe that Jonathan was showing good faith to David. On the other hand, this could be another place where later scribes somewhat miscopied the text, and our account may be missing important details (the books of Samuel have a large number of apparent or possible scribal errors).

In the conversation, Jonathan made a strong case in David's defense. David had never shown disloyalty to Saul or given any signs of maneuvering to gain the crown. Instead, he valiantly fought the Philistines and was legitimately a national hero. Saul himself benefited from David's military prowess and celebrated his achievements. If Saul were to kill David, he would shed "innocent blood," a grave offense against God (vv. 4–5). Saul, who was lucid for this conversation, saw the truth of Jonathan's argument and swore a binding oath in God's name not to harm David. For a time, all was good (vv. 6–7).

Again, we come upon an unspecified extent of time in the narrative. War between Israel and Philistia was renewed, and David again won many victories (v. 8). Saul should have been elated; his program of gradually eradicating all traces of Philistine power inside Israel was moving forward. But once again, his old fear and jealousy began to stir.

The episode at verses 9 and 10 was a repetition of 18:10–11: David was playing the lyre at court when Saul abruptly hurled a spear at him and narrowly missed him. This time, David immediately fled to his home and was apparently in some confusion about what to do next. His wife Michal, who understood how violently unstable her father had become, warned him to flee that very night. Knowing that the front of the house might be watched, she lowered him from a rear window (vv. 11–12; Israelite houses of the time generally had only one exterior door, and the family living quarters were on the second floor).

Michal then took a household idol, evidently something like a bust, and set it in the bed with a goat hair cloth on top to look like David's head and hair; she evidently made up the rest of the bed to look like his body covered by a blanket. She informed men from Saul that David was sick and could not get up (vv. 13–14). It seems that they intended to lure him out and kill him in some secluded place instead of murdering him in his own house in front of his wife. This subterfuge may seem pointless since David was already gone, but Michal's intent was probably to delay the discovery of David's flight as long as possible to give him more time to get away. When Saul heard his men's report, he demanded that they drag him out of bed so that Saul could personally put him to death, but to their chagrin, they discovered that Michal had tricked them (vv. 15–16).

Michal's actions in saving her husband were commendable. She showed a lack of character, however, when she excused her actions to Saul by saying David had threatened to kill her (v. 17). This only further convinced Saul that David was a dangerous threat to himself and his family. She should have, like Jonathan, plucked up her courage and confronted Saul to his face. As the story progresses, she becomes increasingly self-serving and unclear about her loyalty.

Modern readers, however, are stunned to discover that there were idols to household gods in David's house. In reality, such things were ubiquitous in Israel at this time, and the Bible is clear that Israelite homes were awash in idols. Household gods were typically minor deities meant to protect the home from harm. We should not assume, however, that everyone who had such items consciously rejected Yahweh as Israel's covenant god. A large number of people who had such shrines would have also firmly believed that Yahweh was Israel's God and that he had brought them out of Egypt, and that they were obligated to serve him. People can be highly inconsistent in their faith! An analogy might be in Orthodox and Catholic homes where people believe in one God and in Jesus Christ, but who also have small shrines to saints. Like their modern counterparts, these Israelites saw no contradiction. We do not know what David's attitude was (the shrine may have belonged to Michal), but he did tolerate it in his home.

Not knowing where else to go, David fled to Samuel at his home in Ramah. This could not be kept a secret, and Saul sent detachments of men to capture David. Three separate groups of men attempted this, and each time they would be seized by a manic spirit and "prophesy."

This, too, is confusing to us, since we assume that prophesying necessarily implies giving a message from God, perhaps including something about the future. But the Hebrew verb for prophesying can also imply a kind of raving. For this reason, ordinary Israelites tended to regard prophets as mad men (2 Kings 9:11). As far as we can tell, the men whom Saul sent, and later Saul himself, did not give any word from God when they prophesied even though the "Spirit of God" came upon them (1 Sam. 19:20); they simply babbled incoherently and were unable to continue with their mission. Saul himself "prophesied" so fervently that he stripped naked and lay exposed for a full day. This, of course, was not normal behavior for a true prophet of God, such as Elijah or Isaiah.

Living It Out

Our character is not tested when doing the right thing is easy. Of the three tests faced by Saul, Jonathan, and Michal, only Jonathan fully passed. Saul utterly failed, and Michal started well but then gave in to fear. Michal's failure, although seemingly slight, was the saddest of all, as it marked the downward path of the rest of her life. When faced with a moral challenge, we must not compromise.

Jonathan's Loyalty

1 Samuel 20:1–17

The Big Picture

One of the greatest tests of humility is when we sense what is God's will, but it involves us losing rather than gaining prestige or position. In this passage, Jonathan must face the reality that Saul and his family, certainly including Jonathan himself, were by God's design destined to lose power.

Digging In

As our story begins, David has plainly had all he can take from Saul. He left Samuel back in Ramah because staying with Samuel was only a short-term solution. He could not expect Samuel to permanently shield him from Saul, and he probably did not want to put the elderly man at risk of reprisal from the king. Somewhere, away from Saul, he managed to meet up with Jonathan. His repetitive questions ("What have I done? What did I do wrong? How have I sinned against your father so that he wants to take my life?") speak of the depth of his exasperation over Saul's treacherous and erratic behavior.

Jonathan, apparently wanting to be loyal to both sides and hoping that a reconciliation could yet be worked out, declared that he was certain Saul had no plans to murder David. If he had, Saul would have told him (1 Sam. 20:2). David, however, was no longer willing to trust Saul, and he replied with the undeniable fact that Saul knew of Jonathan's loyalty and very likely would conceal from him a plot to murder David. David's dire statement, "As surely as the LORD lives and as you yourself live, there is but a step between me and death" (v. 3), meant that David considered Saul's hostility to be implacable and that should he ever allow himself to fall into Saul's hands, his life was over. Yielding to the force of David's reasoning, Jonathan promised to do whatever David required of him (v. 4).

David then proposed a simple test. The new moon was about to begin. This was the beginning of the month in the Israelite (lunar) calendar, and it took on far more importance than we might have expected (Num. 10:10; 28:11). It would be the occasion for a regular banquet for court members at the royal palace, with attendance being mandatory. David, of course, would not be going, as he fully expected Saul to try to kill him. Jonathan would excuse David on the grounds that he had to go to a family sacrificial meal in Bethlehem. Jonathan could gauge Saul's attitude from his response. If he was satisfied and showed no concern, he was (at least at that moment) not hostile to David. If he went into a rage, this would show that he was frustrated at not being able to capture and kill him. This was far more effective than simply asking Saul what his intentions were toward David. He could always lie in response to such a direct question, but he would not be nearly so on guard about his own disposition. David then appealed to Jonathan again for help, first invoking the covenant the two men had made with each other (1 Sam. 18:3), and then declaring that if Jonathan harbored any fears that David was plotting against the king, he should just cut down David himself (1 Sam. 20:8). Such strong language indicates that David was emotionally at the end of his rope. For his part, Jonathan emphatically asserted that he had no suspicion about David and that he would inform him of any new plot from the king.

Jonathan declared with a strong oath that he would give David an accurate account of Saul's state of mind. David would know if Saul was still implacably hostile and could permanently go on the run, never returning to the royal court (vv. 11–13). We should observe that David did not promise to come back to court if Jonathan brought a favorable report. From what David had seen, Saul had become dangerously erratic and unpredictable, the only constant being his regular loss of control and repeated attempts to spear the young David.

One thing in Jonathan's speech is striking, however: He expected that David would eventually win. "If I continue to live, show me kindness from the LORD, but if I die, don't ever withdraw your kindness from my household—not even when the LORD cuts off every one of David's enemies from the face of the earth" (vv. 14–15). He also renewed his covenant with David (v. 16). Jonathan plainly thought that in this struggle David would rise and Saul, along with his whole household, would fall. Jonathan knew what this implied: he would probably die along with his father. In fact, he all but openly declared that he expected David to become the next king. What could account for this?

We do not know when but it had widely become known that Samuel had anointed David to become king. At first, it was a secret. When Saul first welcomed David into his court, he obviously had no idea that Samuel had named him as Saul's successor. On the other hand, we have indications that at some later time David's destiny was common knowledge even among people in remote locations. When David moved to kill Nabal for his treachery, Abigail, Nabal's wife, met him on the way and persuaded David to turn back. She said, "When the LORD does for my lord all the good he promised you and appoints you ruler over Israel, there will not be remorse or a troubled conscience for my lord because of needless bloodshed or my lord's revenge" (1 Sam. 25:30–31). Abigail lived in a fairly isolated corner of southern Judah, and yet she knew that David was destined to become king. Jonathan, who lived in the center of the court and heard all its gossip, surely learned about David far before Abigail did. In addition, Jonathan knew that Samuel had told Saul that his dynasty would not survive him and that his kingship was forfeited. Jonathan knew that David had not been treacherous against Saul and his family, but he was no fool. He surely knew that David, and not himself, would succeed Saul.

This implies that Jonathan had done something Saul himself could not do: he had accepted God's verdict against the house of Saul. Rather than resist David, Jonathan only sought assurance that David would not eradicate his family when he came to power. He was loyal to his family but subordinate to God's will.

Living It Out

Jonathan did not betray his father, but he did acknowledge that his father and his family were destined to lose the crown. God had spoken, and the man God had chosen was a man Jonathan could not hate. Jonathan did what few men in the Old Testament managed to achieve; he maintained his honor and faith to the end. We must not demand any honor, power, or position that God has not chosen to give us. Otherwise, we follow the path of Saul and not of Jonathan.

Jonathan's Eyes Opened

1 Samuel 20:18–42

The Big Picture

In this passage, Jonathan learns the painful truth that his father has a bizarre but extreme hatred for David and that there is no possibility of healing the rift between the two men. Worse, he will see Saul's insanity and his fury on full display, as his father goes from placid calm to a profane, cursing rage, and finally tries to kill his own son. He surely knew before this that Saul was not well, but his father probably had been a great hero and role model for him. It would be very hard for him when confronted with the full reality of his father's condition.

Digging In

First Samuel 20:18 may strike us as needlessly repetitive; we already know that Jonathan would sound out Saul at the New Moon banquet (see vv. 5–7). Such repetition is a common feature of Hebrew narrative, however. It recapitulates part of the prior part of the text so that the reader does not get lost. Also, in ancient Israel the vast majority of people were not "readers" at all but listeners to an oral recitation; they needed this kind of recapitulation of events in order to follow the thread of the story.

Jonathan then laid out the procedure whereby he would inform David of how things stood. They were apparently in the countryside near Saul's home city, Gibeah. We have already seen how the Israelites tended to name prominent elements of the landscape, such as the two pillar-like rocks at Michmash (1 Sam. 14:4). It appears that there was a conspicuous stone nearby that the locals called "Ezel" (1 Sam. 20:19), and Jonathan wanted David to station himself behind it at the time of their meeting (on the other hand, it is possible that the original text actually said, "over near that heap of stones" and lacked a proper name, "Ezel"). At any rate, Jonathan would shoot three arrows in that direction and send a servant to retrieve them. If Jonathan told the servant he had gone past the arrows and should come back, that was a sign that David could come back to Saul's court. If Jonathan said that the servant had to go further out to find the arrows, that was a sign that David had to get away. It was a simple, coded message, and Jonathan was evidently concerned that he may not be able to speak to David at all (perhaps because witnesses might be present).

At the new moon meal, Saul sat at his regular place with his back to the wall. For security reasons, his back would not be exposed, and it was also unseemly for any guests to be facing the king's back. Two seats immediately beside the king were those of Jonathan, the crown prince, and Abner, the commander of the army. David's seat was evidently right next to theirs, a mark of how high his rank was at court. Remarkably, Saul was unconcerned with David's absence, supposing that he was missing because he was ritually unclean (v. 26). In ancient Israel, there were an enormous number of reasons one might be ritually unclean. Uncleanness was for the most part not for moral reasons and being unclean was no disgrace. But someone in that status could not partake of a sacrificial meal. Saul's quiet supposition that David was absent for purely ritual reasons suggests that he was at that moment not in one of his murderous moods and had even forgotten that David had good reason to be deathly afraid of him. Clearly, Saul was mentally unhinged.

The next day, however, Saul's dark mood returned, and he demanded to know why David did not show up. Jonathan gave his prepared excuse, that David was attending a sacrificial meal in Bethlehem. Saul was having none of it; he was certain (and correct) that Jonathan was trying to protect David. He let forth a tirade of curses against Jonathan, calling him first the "son of a perverse and rebellious woman" and then claiming that his behavior has dishonored his mother (v. 30). In calling Jonathan the son of a rebellious woman, Saul meant that he was by nature rebellious and perverse in his siding with David instead of his own family (Saul was not really attacking the moral character of his wife). In calling him a disgrace to his mother (in the Hebrew, he calls him a disgrace to his mother's nakedness), he meant that Jonathan gave his mother reason to be ashamed that she had given birth to such a bad son. For Saul, Jonathan's duty was clear: he should have joined his father in trying to kill David. The furious Saul threw another spear, this one at Jonathan, but again he missed. The astonished and angry Jonathan now knew that there were no hopes for peaceful relations between Saul and David (vv. 32–34).

The next day, Jonathan made his way back to the place where David was hiding and shot his arrows according to the prearranged signal. Apparently, no one else was in the vicinity, however, and there was no real need for clandestine signals. Jonathan simply dismissed the boy who had retrieved his arrows in order to have a private conversation with David. The two men came together to make their farewells.

David bowed three times to Jonathan. He was still David's superior in rank and Israel's crown prince. Also, David was profoundly grateful to Jonathan. He had been faithful to David and to the truth at the risk of appearing disloyal in the eyes of his father; it had been an enormous sacrifice. The two men kissed, a common form of greeting or farewell in Israel, and wept. Ancient customs are quite different from those of modern America. Kissing in public was never done between husband and wife because, between a couple, it was regarded as a prelude to sexual activity and therefore crude. Kissing between friends, however, was not sexual and therefore not frowned upon. Also, it was no shame for men to weep publicly when in great distress. It was thought to be entirely natural, like smiling when one was happy. Jonathan then reminded David of the covenant they had made and reminded him that Yahweh was a witness to that covenant. It was not that he did not trust David, but he was sure that David would eventually have all the power, and he wanted to be sure that his own children would be safe.

Living It Out

In a sense, Jonathan lost two of the people he most loved in the course of two days. The man he once knew his father to be was morally and emotionally gone, and his best friend was on a path that he could not follow if he was to do his duty. But Jonathan did what was right, faithfully carrying out his obligations to both men. It is painful to see someone whom we have loved and respected degraded by sin. Jonathan shows us that even in the face of such pain, we can still carry on and do the right thing.

David's Deceit

1 Samuel 21:1–6

The Big Picture

David, son-in-law of the king and hero of Israel, was now a desperate fugitive on the run for his life. He had nothing but his wits to sustain him. In desperation, he quickly resorted to deceit in order to avoid suspicion in his encounters with people along the way.

Digging In

David was now entirely alone. He had no food, no weapon, and no companions. Ahimelech observed with some surprise that David was alone in verse 1, and he was obviously alone in Gath at the presence of Achish, king of Gath, when he pretended to be insane (1 Sam. 21:13; he could hardly pull off pretending to be a mindless mental case if he was accompanied by a band of followers). David told Ahimelech he had some companions stationed elsewhere (v. 2), but this was plainly a lie. David for the first time attracts companions to himself in the next chapter.

Surprisingly, however, Jesus appears to imply that David really did have companions when he spoke of the incident, when the Pharisees challenged Jesus about the disciples plucking grain on the Sabbath. He said, "Haven't you read what David and those who were with him did when he was hungry—how he entered the house of God and took and ate the bread of the Presence, which is not lawful for any but the priests to eat? He even gave some to those who were with him" (Luke 6:3–4). But Jesus's words should be understood as part of a rabbinical disputation rather than simple narrative concerned primarily with historical details. As far as the priest Ahimelech knew, David did have companions, and he made a ruling allowing David's companions to eat the holy bread. Thus, for the purposes of the rabbinical dispute, the companions were a legal reality and they were authorized to eat the bread, establishing the precedent that Jesus cites. It was important for Jesus to cite this precedent, that the priest had ruled that the companions could eat the holy bread, because Jesus was being attacked for allowing his companions, the disciples, to pluck grain on the Sabbath.

Nob was located south of Saul's city of Gibeah and north of Jerusalem (Jerusalem at this time was not an Israelite city; it was occupied by the Jebusites). The central sanctuary of Israel had been at Shiloh, but it had been destroyed by the Philistines. The ark of the covenant went from place to place after the Philistines captured and returned it; it seems to have been, for the most part, in Saul's custody. We do not know if the shrine at Nob was regarded as the new central sanctuary or if it was simply a shrine to which worshipers went to sacrifice. With the earlier central sanctuary at Shiloh destroyed and the priests scattered, and because the ark of the covenant was moving about with whoever controlled it, the religious life of Israel at this time was highly confused. Eventually, David and then Solomon would set things in order so that Israel's religious life would again function with a single, central shrine, just as the Law required. But at Nob, it is at least clear that the priests were legitimate; Ahimelech was the great-grandson of Eli.

It seems unlikely that David deliberately headed to Nob. He probably simply headed south in his flight from Saul and happened upon Nob and thought that this would be a good place to get some supplies. Ahimelech was wholly ignorant of the conflict between Saul and David, and he accepted, without question, David's lie that he was on a secret mission for Saul. Since David was a fugitive, he needed as much food as he could carry with him and asked for five loaves of bread, implying that it was for him and his companions.

The sanctuary contained an altar for the "Bread of the Presence." Twelve small loaves of this bread would be set out every sabbath as an offering before God, and only the priests could eat it (Lev. 24:5–9). By the strict letter of the law, therefore, there seemed no possibility of allowing David to take this bread. Ahimelech, however, ruled that David and his companions could eat it as long as they had not been with a woman, that is, had not recently had sexual intercourse. Priests routinely made rulings about what was permitted or not permitted under Israelite laws (see, for example, Hag. 2:11–13). To this day, rabbinical bodies make kosher rulings.

Uncleanness was not a moral matter; it was a matter of ritual cleanness (a man would be ritually unclean even if his sexual encounter had been with his wife). Sexual activity was one of many things that could render a person unclean, and that person had to go through ritual cleansing in order to be allowed to participate in holy things, such as a sacrifice. We should note that the Law does not imply that there was something defiling about women as such; both men and women were made unclean by sexual activity, and it was the male emission, not the female body, that was defiling (Lev. 15:18). David asserted that he always made sure his men were "consecrated" (ritually clean) when they went out on a mission. Many Israelites regarded going out to wage war as part of the "army of the living God" as a holy matter, requiring the troops to be ritually clean. The Law does not require that Israelite soldiers be ritually clean, but David said that he nonetheless demanded it of the men under his command. Since David lies repeatedly in this narrative, we do not know if this claim was true.

We have seen a great deal of deceit and misdirection in 1 Samuel. God himself commanded Samuel to tell people he had come to Bethlehem to make a sacrifice when his real purpose was to anoint a new king (1 Sam. 16:2–3). Jonathan, similarly, lied to his father about why David had not attended the new moon meal (1 Sam. 20:28–29). We observed earlier (Day Twenty-Two) that deceiving a corrupt government bent on committing murder was not evil. David's deceit of

Ahimelech, however, is impossible to justify. Ahimelech was not in any way involved in the plot to murder David, and David had no right to lie to him and in so doing, drag him into the conflict between himself and Saul. Although David had no way of knowing it, this would have disastrous results for the priests at Nob. The rare, exceptional cases allowing for deception, such as Samuel's claim that his purpose in coming to Bethlehem was to make a sacrifice, are precisely that: rare and exceptional. Although we speak with hindsight, David should have avoided Nob altogether, trusting that God would provide for him in some other way.

Living It Out

Very few of us are likely to find ourselves in a situation where we have to mislead Nazi SS members on the hunt for Jews. Our rule should be that lying is wrong and has unforeseen and always bad consequences. David's situation does, however, show us something of the human condition. When the world is filled with violence and cruelty, even the innocent parties, such as David, become desperate. They find it very difficult to do the right thing. This, too, should be a warning to us, lest the evil around us overcome us.

Saul's Atrocity

1 Samuel 21:7–22:23

The Big Picture

This chapter records one of the darkest episodes of 1 Samuel, the slaughter of the priests of Nob. It also introduces us to one of the most despicable characters of the Old Testament, Doeg the Edomite. This man was so vile that an entire Psalm was written to excoriate him, Psalm 52. David said of him, "You love any words that destroy, / you treacherous tongue! // This is why God will bring you down forever. / He will take you, ripping you out of your tent; / he will uproot you from the land of the living" (Ps. 52:4–5).

Digging In

One of Saul's men, a certain Edomite named Doeg, happened to be at the shrine at Nob while David was there. David knew and recognized Doeg at the shrine (1 Sam. 22:22), but at the time, he gave little thought to the possible consequences of him being a witness to the events that followed. But Doeg saw that Ahimelech gave David provisions and, most ominously, the sword of Goliath. Ahimelech's arming of David would convince Saul that he had taken David's side in the conflict, and the sword was apparently magnificent; "There's none like it!" David said (1 Sam. 21:9). In Saul's mind, Ahimelech had given David one of the best weapons in Israel!

In a side story, David fled to the Philistine city of Gath (vv. 10–15). This, it would seem, was the last place on earth to which he should have gone, as David had no greater enemies than the Philistines. He apparently hoped he would not be recognized and that he would be safe there, since Saul could not possibly follow him into Philistine territory. But David was caught. It was a crazy idea, and he got away by pretending to be insane. We, at least, learn from the account that Achish, King of Gath, had a good sense of humor. He already had all the crazy people he could use (v. 15)!

David made his way to a hideout in Adullam, in the Shephelah southwest of Bethlehem—a fairly remote location. David's family were among the first to join him, probably because they were in danger from Saul. David, however, was an extraordinarily popular and gifted man, and the conflict between him and Saul soon became common knowledge. Most people, naturally, would want to stay on the sidelines and out of trouble. But people who had nothing to lose (those who were "desperate, in debt, or discontented," according to 1 Sam. 22:2), soon found their way to him. We should not romanticize these men, as though they were all the righteous and unlawfully oppressed. But under David's leadership, this ragtag bunch became a cohesive and valiant unit, the core of David's future army.

The king of Moab gave sanctuary to David's parents, an urgent matter since his parents were too old to live as fugitives on the run (vv. 3–4). We do not know why the Moabite king did this. We know from Ruth that Jesse had Moabite blood, and this may have influenced the king's decision. Also, the king may have suspected that David's star was rising, and Saul's was falling. For a while, David stayed in Moab at a place called "the stronghold."

At some point, a prophet named Gad joined David's force and told David to return from Moab to Judah. David went to the "forest of Hereth," a place mentioned only here (v. 5). It was probably just south of Adullam.

The narrative suddenly shifts back to Saul's court, where he is once again under a tree (this time a tamarisk, but previously a pomegranate; see 1 Sam. 14:2). Saul made a bitter speech filled with pathetic self-pity and paranoia. He accused everyone of conspiring against him, thinking that they expected David to reward them with high offices. This self-centered tirade gave Doeg the perfect opportunity to gain Saul's favor by giving him the information that, up until now, he had kept to himself. Right when Saul thinks that nobody loves him, Doeg demonstrates his loyalty! Doeg told Saul that he saw Ahimelech give David food and, most ominously, a great sword.

It is surprising that Ahimelech "inquired of the LORD" for David (1 Sam. 22:10), since he made the inquiry in ignorance of the true circumstances of David's flight (verse 14 shows that until he came before Saul, Ahimelech had no idea that David was on the run from Saul). Perhaps David's inquiry was something very vague, such as, "Will I have success in my current business?" But the act would have made it appear that Ahimelech knew and supported David's true purpose.

The paranoid Saul was convinced that Ahimelech had joined a conspiracy to replace him with David. He summoned the priests of Nob to stand before him. Poor Ahimelech, both terrified and bewildered, responded that as far as he knew, David was among Saul's most loyal soldiers. Saul was unmoved by this excuse and ordered all the priests to be put to death. Saul's regular troops, however, were mortified at this command and refused to carry it out (v. 17).

Doeg and his men were not nearly so scrupulous. They killed the "eighty-five men who wore linen ephods" (that is, all the priests of Nob), and then made their way to Nob itself, where they slaughtered every living thing: "both men and women, infants and nursing babies, oxen, donkeys, and sheep" (v. 19). Saul, who had been unwilling to carry out a *ḥerem* against the Amalekites, completed a *ḥerem* against a peaceful town of Israelite priests. This calamity can be viewed in part as a fulfillment of the curse laid on the family of Eli (1 Sam. 3:11–14), but this does not make it any less of an atrocity or make the guilt of Saul and Doeg any less great.

One man, Abiathar son of Ahimelech, did escape and made his way to David, where he found sanctuary (1 Sam. 22:22–23; we learn at 23:6 that Abiathar met up with David while the latter was on a campaign against the Philistines). David, with good reason, blamed himself for the debacle (to his credit, he did not excuse or cover up how his actions had brought this about).

Living It Out

The existence of cruel, sociopathic evil is a hard fact of human existence. Another hard fact is this: when society becomes corrupt, such evil men rise to the top. As Christians, we are not to hate and fear the world, but we are to recognize that evil is real; it is not the concoction of an overactive imagination. We need God's guidance to recognize true evil when it appears among us.

David's Wilderness Years

1 Samuel 23:1–29

The Big Picture

In this passage, David faces bitter betrayal twice, first from the men of Keilah and then from the men of Ziph. Constantly on the run, and with people from Judah, his own tribe, turning against him, he had to have been profoundly discouraged. In the middle of all this, Jonathan showed up with what was in effect a word from God.

Digging In

The city of Keilah was just south of Adullam, one of David's early hiding places, and thus he would have known the area well. Also, being on the edge of the Shephelah, in the border area between Judah and Philistia, it was a natural spot for the Philistines to attack. Informed of the Philistine assault on the town, David decided to assist the city after receiving affirmation from God that this was the right course of action. His small army, understandably, did not feel they were ready to take on the Philistines, but a second confirmation from God fixed the decision in David's mind. All we are told of the battle is that David won, plundered the Philistines, and rescued Keilah (1 Sam. 23:1–5).

David's frequent recourse to asking God for direction is a prominent feature of this chapter. This creates a contrast with Saul, whom God had ceased to answer (1 Sam. 14:37). We naturally wonder how David inquired of God and how God answered. It may be that David took his questions to the prophet Gad, who after a time came back with an answer. This seems especially likely with the answer given in verse 4, because God's answer in that verse is quite full: "Go at once to Keilah, for I will hand the Philistines over to you" (1 Sam. 23:4).

Verse 6, however, tells us that when Abiathar son of Ahimelech joined David at Keilah, he had the "ephod" with him. This was an important part of the priestly vestments, a garment that appears to have been something like a vest. Most importantly, it carried a pouch that had within it the Urim and Thummim (Exod. 28:27–30), the mysterious stones used for seeking an answer from God. After Abiathar's arrival, when David wanted an answer, he said, "Bring the ephod" (v. 9). The important thing was not the ephod itself but the Urim and Thummim. We do not know how the stones worked. The simplest proposal is that they were flat, like two coins, and would be tossed when seeking an answer. Putting it in our terms, two "heads" meant "yes," two "tails" meant "no," and one head and one tail meant, "no answer." Whether this is precisely right or not, we observe that the questions David asked God are "yes or no" questions: "Will Saul come down as your servant has heard?" (v. 11), and "Will the citizens of Keilah hand me and my men over to Saul?" (v. 12).

God told David that yes, Saul would come for him, and yes, the men of Keilah would betray him to Saul. Keilah was evidently a walled city, and David had taken up residence there. While this seemed to offer protection, it was a trap, because a walled city could easily be surrounded and besieged. Saul recognized this and began to move against David, although he was suffering under the delusion that God was on his side (v. 7). By telling us how God had forewarned David that he would be betrayed by Keilah, the narrative indicates that Saul was badly mistaken. David abandoned the city and Saul lost his opportunity. He fled to the rugged area of Ziph, in the southern part of Judah, where he thought that Saul would find pursuit difficult (vv. 13–14).

While we naturally despise the gross ingratitude of the people of Keilah, we should at least consider two factors. First, Saul had been their king a long time, and some no doubt sincerely believed that he was legitimate and that David was a rebel. Second, if they were trapped in the city under siege and facing starvation, the easiest solution would be to hand over David's head to Saul (for comparison, note what happened to the rebel Sheba according to 2 Sam. 20:14–22).

Jonathan suddenly reappears in the narrative (vv. 16–18). We are not told how, but he found David when Saul could not. The account is very brief, but it contains several important points. First, Jonathan encouraged David at a time when the latter may have been at wit's end and ready to flee as far from Israel as possible (as v. 15 may imply). Second, Jonathan explicitly asserted his belief that David would be the next king, something he only obliquely stated earlier (20:14–15). Indeed, he said, even his father knew that David was destined to win. Besides being a personal encouragement to David, this showed that many people knew about David's anointing and support for him was becoming widespread. Third, Jonathan expressed his hope that he would live to be David's second-in-command. Tragically, this did not happen; Jonathan died in battle alongside his father. One can only wonder if the reign of David would have been far better if he had only had the steady and loyal hand of Jonathan to guide him. Fourth, they made yet another covenant, although in truth it was a renewal of the two previous covenants they had made. Jonathan only makes one more brief appearance in the story, when he is killed by the Philistines (1 Sam. 31:2). When Jonathan left David this time, as far as we know, he never saw him again.

Once again, however, David faced the prospect of being handed over to Saul by the local population. It appears that the people of Keilah did not preemptively plan to betray David to Saul; God merely informed David that when they were faced with the prospect of a siege, they would yield. Some Ziphites, however, actively sought to win Saul's favor by delivering David to him. Saul remained fixedly in denial about how God had turned against him, and he blessed the men of Ziph in the Lord's name (1 Sam. 23:21). After the Ziphites had tracked David and reported his movements to Saul, the king set out to close the trap. Because of the military intelligence supplied by his Ziphite spies, he was able to maneuver into a position from which David and his men could not escape. Suddenly, a messenger arrived. The Philistines, taking advantage of Saul being in the far south of Israel, launched a major attack and were plundering the country. Saul could not ignore this, and he broke off the attack and turned back. Once again, contrary to Saul's thinking, God was working for David and against Saul.

Living It Out

We might think of Jonathan as David's Barnabas, a man of encouragement sent by God at the right time to rescue God's chosen man from despair in the face of opposition. Christians are subject to dismay and disillusion when the opposition set against them seems too strong, and they need a Jonathan to come alongside and provide a reminder of God's call, purpose, and certain victory. More than that, we all need to be a Jonathan to other believers, especially for those facing persecution.

Day Thirty-Three

David's Loyalty

1 Samuel 24:1–22

The Big Picture

This passage tells us of a crisis in the life of David. On a superficial reading, it appears not to be a crisis but an opportunity. David could end Saul's life and, literally with one fell swoop, put an end to the threat to his own life and put himself in a position to become king. It all looked very easy. In fact, it was *too* easy. Killing Saul would prove to many Israelites that David was what Saul always said he was: an opportunistic rebel, bent on achieving power by any means. David would have to choose to take the "high road" and not strike out against the king. He would need to prove to himself and to his nation that he was a man of principle and that his elevation to the throne had been a work of God and not the work of a scheming insubordinate. The crisis was when David, knife in hand, stood behind Saul and had to decide what to do.

Digging In

The wilderness of En-gedi is a beautiful, wooded ravine on the west side of the Dead Sea. Now an Israeli national park (called Ein Gedi), it is a very popular area for hiking and wildlife observation. Visitors can view the magnificent David Waterfall, named for the king who, for a time, resided here. The name En-gedi means, "Spring of the Goat-kid," a typical name for local areas. The text mentions another site at En-gedi named "Rocks of the Wild Goats." En-gedi has abundant water, wildlife for hunting, and foliage, but it is within the Judean desert, isolated by very harsh terrain. Thus, it was an excellent hideout for David and his men.

Saul, having dealt with the Philistine incursion, resumed his pursuit of David. Local informants, it seems, relayed to him the information that David was at En-gedi, and taking along a relatively small group of his best warriors, Saul made the hard trip south. The terrain of the En-gedi ravine is quite rugged, with crevices and caves in the cliff faces. Saul went into one of these to relieve himself, using a cave both for privacy and security. This particular cave was much deeper than he imagined, however, and David and a group of his men were in the back (David did not necessarily have all of the private army with him in the cave). The inclusion of the uncomfortable detail that the episode occurred when Saul went to relieve himself (the Hebrew uses a euphemism: Saul went into the cave to "cover his feet") is surprising; the text could have just said that he went into the cave without mentioning this fact. It may be that the author wants to stress both Saul's vulnerability and also his loss of dignity. Saul was extremely proud at this point in his life, and he was determined to hold the crown. Here, however, the narrator lets us see him in the most embarrassing and private of predicaments.

David's men naturally saw this as a literal Godsend: Yahweh had delivered David's enemy into his hand, and David could strike him down. They knew—as David did—that this was a fight to the death. From their point of view, killing Saul was the only rational thing to do, and God had arranged things so that David could do precisely that.

David first crept up and cut off a part of Saul's cloak; the king had evidently hung it up on a rock somewhere behind him. Why David did this is unclear; one would think he would either kill Saul outright or do nothing. Later, he did make use of the cutoff portion of Saul's cloak to prove that he could have killed him if he had wanted to, but that does not seem to have been his initial motivation, since his "conscience bothered him because he had cut off the corner of Saul's robe" (1 Sam. 24:5). Perhaps he had initially conceived of cutting off part of the cloak as something like a prank on Saul, and this was what later pricked his conscience.

At any rate, David quickly realized that for him, killing Saul was out of the question, and he told his men that he would allow no such thing. The phrase in verse 7 translated as "David persuaded his men" could be rendered, "David tore apart his men," meaning that he rebuked them in strong terms. Saul, meanwhile, ignorant of how his life had hung in the balance, made his way out of the cave. As soon as Saul was far enough away that he and his men could not easily apprehend David, and yet close enough for shouted communication to still be possible, David emerged and announced himself to the astonished king.

It is important to grasp that David fully understood that he was destined to be king and that there was no way that this would occur while Saul still lived. He also understood that Saul was doing everything in his power to kill him. And although David had great faith, his faith was not so perfect that he could not give in to fear and despair, as we shall see. Therefore, David's determination to do the right thing and not kill Saul was all the more remarkable. A man of less integrity would have cut Saul's throat. But David, rather than take Saul's life himself, chose to allow God, in his own way and time, to remove Saul. Although Saul regarded David as an outlaw, David would not behave like one. He would, of course, keep his distance from Saul but would not actively seek his death or downfall.

David's actions and words reflect this conviction (vv. 8–19). He bowed to Saul, whom he still regarded as his legitimate king. He proved that he had the opportunity to kill Saul but did not take it. He implicitly rebuked Saul for seeking to kill him, but he declared that God would be the judge in this matter and not David. He declared himself to be a "dead dog" or a "flea" (v. 14) and not a dangerous enemy seeking to overthrow the king. Saul, in a brief moment of sanity, realized that David had done nothing wrong and even that David was chosen by God and therefore destined to win. Like Jonathan, he even appealed to David to preserve his family after he took the crown (vv. 20–22; see 20:15). But of course, Saul's clarity was short-lived. He should have made public plans to turn the crown over to David, but instead, he soon resumed the hunt for David's life. In the end, Saul's family would be almost entirely annihilated—and not by David but by God.

Living It Out

Not every opportunity is from God. If something is there for the taking, we tend to think, we ought to take it. But God never gives us the right thing in the wrong way. We must never allow a theological-sounding reason to overrule basic principles of right and wrong. We must never say, "God dropped this in my lap, so it must be okay."

Abigail's Intercession

1 Samuel 25:1–44

The Big Picture

We should not imagine that David was the placid saint we might see portrayed in stained-glass windows. He had integrity and he loved God, but he was also a passionate and impulsive man. In this chapter, his inner furies got the best of him, but fortunately, there was a woman on hand to enable him to come to his senses.

Digging In

The death of Samuel (1 Sam. 25:1) has little direct bearing on the story of this chapter, but his passing was too momentous an event for the narrator to pass over in silence. The event does mark, however, that the old order of the judges was well and truly dead. Israel, now with the two titanic figures of Saul and David facing off against each other, was firmly set on the path of monarchy.

Maon (v. 2) was a town in the far south of Judah. The "Carmel" mentioned here is the hill country in the vicinity of Maon; it is not the famous Mount Carmel on the Mediterranean coast, the place where Elijah had his confrontation with the prophets of Baal (1 Kings 18:19–40). Nabal was a prosperous sheep owner who lived in the region; he had so many sheep that that he hired a number of shepherds to look after his flocks. This being a harsh, barren country, the shepherds would take the sheep from place to place in search of pasture. Nabal was a severe businessman, both greedy and arrogant. His wife, Abigail, was beautiful but also sensible; the Hebrew literally says she was "good of prudence." It evidently was not a good marriage, at least for her.

To understand the background to this story, we should realize that the hill country of Judah was something like the "wild west" with its "open prairie" in the early years of the American west. Shepherds, far removed from anything like civilization or the protection of a local militia, were at the mercy of roving bands of outlaws who would steal sheep and cattle at any opportunity. Beyond simple banditry, these gangs were often composed of men from different ethnic groups (such as the Amalekites) and had absolutely no sense of moral obligation regarding those whom they plundered. Even fellow Israelites could resort to thievery. This being the case, shepherds and their livestock desperately needed some form of local protection—some sense of law and order. For Nabal's shepherds, David's men provided just that. It does not appear that David and Nabal had entered into a formal agreement, whereby David's men would protect the livestock from raiders in return for a specified cut of the profits at shearing season. But Nabal, who would not have been ignorant of the circumstances of his men and their sheep, would have known about the presence of David's men and the protection they provided. Also, there were probably plenty of friendly exchanges between Nabal's men and David's. The shepherds knew well that they were under David's protection and would be expected to give some kind of compensation.

This was the situation when shearing time came and David sent messengers to Nabal. With the shearing of the sheep, the wool would be sold and Nabal could have easily afforded to give David's men payment for services rendered. This was a barter economy, and payment could have been made in the form of livestock, clothing, food supplies, or precious metals (gold or silver but not coinage, which had not yet been invented). David did not have a contract with Nabal (and thus he did not come to Nabal with specific demands), but he was operating under something analogous to the "code of the west." He had treated his neighbor well, and so Nabal in turn should treat him well. David's request was simple and tactful: "Please give whatever you have on hand to your servants and to your son David" (v. 8).

Nabal refused David's request with a series of harsh but hollow excuses. He claimed to not know who David was, when in fact he knew a great deal about him. He classified David as a rebel and a thief, when in fact David had protected Nabal's wealth from thieves. He claimed he could not afford to give David's men anything when in fact he had enjoyed a very prosperous year thanks to the protection David had given. Nabal clearly knew that custom and decency demanded that he show David's men some appreciation, but his mean and greedy spirit vented itself upon them with lies, mockery, and a harsh refusal (vv. 10–11). David was furious at this treatment; with four hundred armed men, he set out to annihilate Nabal and the men who served him (vv. 12–13).

Abigail understood how the world worked much better than her arrogant husband. She knew that a body of warriors would not take such insults lightly and that the lives of everyone on Nabal's estate hung in the balance. She hastily put together a supply of food sufficient for a banquet for David's men, loaded them on donkeys, and rushed to intercept David's company of fighting men. She fell on her face before David and pled for the lives of the men on her estate.

She made several important points. First, David should realize that he had not been singled out for bad treatment; Nabal treated everyone that way. There is a Hebrew word *nabal*; it is often translated "fool" or "stupid," but it does not mean that the person is gullible or unintelligent. A better translation would be "jerk," since it refers to a person who is arrogant, mean, and utterly selfish. And so, she said, "His name means 'stupid,' and stupidity is all he knows" (v. 25). Second, she said that she hoped that he would accept the food she brought as sufficient compensation for David's services (vv. 27–28). Third, she declared that she was certain that David would triumph over Saul and become the next king (v. 29–30). Fourth, she asserted that it would be a terrible blemish on David when he rose to power if he had "needless bloodshed" on his hands. David worked hard to maintain his integrity before God and men, and he should not throw that away now in a fit of anger (vv. 30–31). Nabal's subordinates, after all, were guiltless, but David in his anger had intended to kill them all.

David saw the wisdom in her words and thanked God that she had been there to stop him from committing an atrocity (vv. 32–35). In the end, he did not need to do anything. Nabal, who at heart was evidently a coward, was so traumatized by the news of how near he had come to losing his head that he had some kind of seizure, lay comatose for ten days, and died. The story's ending is both ironic and satisfactory; Nabal, who did not want to give David anything, ended up losing his wife to David (vv. 39–44)!

Living It Out

We often let our baser emotions get control of us, especially when we have been wronged. David's anger was such that he nearly committed mass murder. But like David, we can be turned away from the baser elements of our nature if we have a godly person on hand to give counsel and display calmness. We should pray that God keeps such people around us and that we listen when they speak.

David's Second Show of Loyalty

1 Samuel 26:1–25

The Big Picture

Resisting a single temptation demonstrates that one has a conscience and desires to do the right thing. However, a single moral victory does not always prove a person's character, especially when the temptation is to something that one especially wants or seems to provide a way out of a difficult situation. One's character is proven only by repeated victories over temptation. A single victory, after all, can be a temporary show of strength by a person who is otherwise weak and vacillating. In this passage, David again has the opportunity, it seems, to put an end to all his troubles by killing Saul. The only thing that might stay his hand is his conviction that Saul is God's anointed and that rebellion against him is rebellion against God. He proves his character by refusing to lay a hand on Saul and does so without any hesitation about what he should do.

Digging In

David was at this time in the region of Ziph, the district in south-ern Judah which contained Maon and Carmel, the places mentioned in the previous chapter. Hachilah was a prominent hill in this area; it was located southeast of the rugged and barren territory called Jeshimon, near the Dead Sea (1 Sam. 23:19 and 26:1).

This passage is obviously similar to chapter 24. In both passages, David was in flight from Saul, who came after him with three thousand elite soldiers. David had an opportunity to kill Saul while he was in a highly vulnerable position, and his men encouraged him to do that very thing. But David refrained from killing him out of respect for the fact that he was Yahweh's anointed, although he did take tokens to prove that he could have killed Saul (the first time, a part of Saul's cloak, and the second time, his spear). In both, David confronted Saul from a distance, saying that others have poisoned his mind against David and that Saul had no good reason to try to pursue him. In both passages, Saul, in response, tearfully spoke of his error and remorse.

Readers naturally wonder how it is that there are two episodes so similar. We should remember that the Bible tells us about only a few events from the many trials and adventures David had in the course of his long career. First and 2 Samuel are, compared to modern biogra-phies, extremely short and selective in the details they provide. Thus, the author has specifically selected these two stories, chapters 24 and 26, for inclusion in the book. Ancient storytellers and audiences, in fact, loved narratives that contained "parallel accounts" (two stories that are very similar). For them, the repetition made for a great story and pointed out that certain episodes were important. In this case, the repetition confirms the fact that David was determined in his mind to not actively rebel against Saul or raise a hand against him, even when he had the perfect opportunity to kill him. If God wanted to make David king, God would do it; David would not push things along by committing violence. Also, David could truthfully say that the hostility of Saul toward David had always been one-sided; David did nothing to deserve it. If David had resisted the temptation once, one might regard that as an exceptional moment, but the repetition shows that David was steadfast in his moral position regarding the king, Yahweh's anointed.

Also, the repetition allows the narrator to bring out different aspects of the two episodes. Apart from the facts that they occurred at different places (the hill of Hachilah in chapter 26, in contrast to the ravine of En-gedi in chapter 24) and that certain details are different (Saul was asleep in the middle of his troops in chapter 26, against being alone in a cave in chapter 24), the words spoken by David and Saul are different in significant ways. In chapter 24, David spoke only to Saul, but in chapter 26, David spoke at length to Abner, the commander of Saul's army. David also complained that Saul was forcing him out of the land of Israel, so that, against his will, he would have to sojourn among pagans (v. 19). He said no such thing in chapter 24. Also, in chapter 24, Saul asked David to swear that he would not harm Saul's family after he became king, and David did so (vv. 21–22). But in chapter 26, Saul asked David to come back to him, but David tacitly refused (vv. 21–22).

David's rebuke of Abner (vv. 15–16) demonstrates his loyalty to Saul. It was truly lax of Saul's commander to fail to post sufficient watches to protect the life of the king during the night. On the other hand, the narrator tells us that God sent a deep sleep on all of Saul's troops (v. 12). It may be that Abner had posted guards, but they, too, fell asleep. Regardless, David's demand that Abner do a better job of protecting Saul is not what one would expect an enemy to say. David's anxiety about having to seek sanctuary among pagans (v. 19) fore-shadows the next chapter, in which he makes himself a vassal of the Philistines.

Saul's request that David come back to him (v. 21) can be read as pure treachery on Saul's part—that he intended to kill David as soon as he could get his hands on him. But based on what we have seen of Saul, it is more likely that the request was sincere. Saul, at the moment he wept and blurted out his remorse over how he had treated David, was thinking he would receive him back as one of his own sons and all would be well. Saul, however, was so emotionally unstable that nothing he said could be trusted. Sooner or later, he would throw another spear at David, and this time, he might hit his target. David wisely kept his distance but not before he had proven that he was a loyal Israelite and subject of the king and that he was leaving the matter in God's hands.

Living It Out

We are all familiar with the besetting sin, a temptation that seems to come to us again and again. Resisting temptation a single time does not create a pattern or habit; it must be refused repeatedly. David, of course, was not here dealing with a typical besetting sin, but he was in a desperate situation and had two unexpected opportunities to escape his trouble by assassinating God's anointed. Those opportunities (that could have easily been interpreted to be gifts from God) created a much stronger temptation than the typical besetting sin. But David proved that if one refusal of temptation showed that he had a moral compass, repeated refusal of the temptation showed that he had integrity and moral strength. For us, whether the temptation is a typical kind we face daily or is of a more unusual kind, the truth remains the same: We show our character only by repeated rejection of temptation.

David's Alliance with the Philistines

1 Samuel 27:1–12

The Big Picture

David was in a desperate situation and felt he had to do something decisive to keep himself and his people alive. Was his decision right or wrong? Were the repercussions of his actions good or evil? The Bible only gives us a bare narration of the events, and it forces us to ponder these questions.

Digging In

The Philistines occupied five major cities in southwestern Canaan near the Mediterranean. These five cities, called the Philistine Pentapolis, were Gath, Ashdod, Ekron, Ashkelon, and Gaza. Each of the cities was ruled by a Philistine warlord, and the five were in a loose confederation that combined their forces for military operations against Israel. Of the five cities, Gath and Ekron were more inland, in the gently sloping terrain called the Shephelah. Gath was south of

Ekron, and thus it was the closest city to the area of southern Judah that David and his men routinely traversed. Therefore, it seems, David chose to flee to Gath because of its location. Of the five, Gath was the most accessible city.

The warlord of Gath was a man named Achish. When David went to him, he clearly put himself and his troops at Achish's disposal, meaning that he became Achish's vassal. This was further confirmed when Achish gave to David the village of Ziklag, located to the south of Gath and closer to territory in which David's little army had previously sojourned. David in effect became the warlord of Ziklag but was in a vassal relationship to Achish of Gath.

What are we to make of David's decision to subordinate himself to a Philistine master? We should not assume that everything he did was right or in accord with God's will. From a strategic point of view, it was questionable, since it played into Saul's contention that David was a traitor and a rebel. David could hardly portray himself as Israel's hope when he was in an alliance with Israel's greatest enemy. One might argue that David's hand was forced by Saul. David could not remain on the run forever. The terrain he inhabited in southern Judah was harsh, and he had to keep his 600 men and their families fed and protected. Recent events had shown that there were people in Judah ready to betray him to Saul (1 Sam. 23:12; 25:10; 26:1). But if he had to flee Israel, did he have to go to the Philistines, at that time Israel's most dangerous and implacable enemy? He could have gone to Moab. He appeared to have been on good terms with the Moabite king, since he had entrusted his parents to the king's care (1 Sam. 22:3–4). In addition, since Moab was on the other side of the Dead Sea, it would have been very difficult for Saul to pursue him there. We should be very careful, however, about making judgments on what David should or should not have done on the basis of the political or military situation. We know very little about the circumstances surrounding his decision, and any arguments we make in favor of one action over another are grounded in ignorance. Instead of proposing alternative solutions based in our very limited knowledge of the situation on the ground at the time, we would do well to pay close attention to what the text of the Bible tells us.

The passage describes David's decision-making process as follows: "One of these days I'll be swept away by Saul. There is nothing better for me than to escape immediately to the land of the Philistines. Then Saul will give up searching for me everywhere in Israel, and I'll escape from him" (1 Sam. 27:1). David gave what seems to have been a realistic appraisal of the situation, but what is entirely lacking is any reference to God. Even though Jonathan, Abigail, and Saul himself had all told David that he was sure to win and become Israel's next king, David seems to have temporarily lost his faith that God would see him through to victory. He does not seem to have taken any reassurance from anointing by Samuel to be the next king. Most significantly, he does not enquire of God for direction, something he had done in the past (1 Sam. 23:2, 10–11). It is astonishing to the reader that David became a vassal of a Philistine warlord; if God had confirmed that this was the right decision, the narrator almost certainly would have told us. The text frames the account in such a way that we can only assume that the decision was David's alone and was made without seeking divine guidance or approval. Like Abraham and Sarah deciding that the only way they could have a son would be if Abraham went to Hagar, David apparently decided that his only option was to flee to Philistia.

David was now serving two masters. On the one hand, he had to convince Achish that he was a loyal vassal and had fully turned against Israel. On the other hand, he had to avoid doing anything that might convince the Israelites that he had truly turned traitor and was now their enemy. He solved the problem by conducting regular raids on the Geshurites, the Girzites, and the Amalekites (the latter group was often hostile to Israel). He took much plunder, and he would have been required to send some of this to his suzerain, Achish. When he did this, he assured Achish that he had despoiled the people of Judah as well as the Jerahmeelites and the Kenites (the Kenites were allies of the Israelites; the Jerahmeelites were either a clan of Judah or a people who were assimilated to Judah). In effect, he claimed to be attacking Israelites when in fact he was attacking Israel's traditional enemies. In order to keep the true nature of his raiding secret, he killed every man and woman in every settlement he plundered.

One might justify David's actions on the grounds that he was continuing the work of the conquest, but the passage explicitly tells us the real reason he killed so many people: so that they would not talk. We cannot say that David, in his attack on the Amalekites, was continuing Saul's campaign and correcting his failure to bring about the Amalekite annihilation. Saul was condemned for keeping the Amalekite livestock as plunder (1 Sam. 15:9), and yet David kept the livestock as well (1 Sam.1 17:9). David was very much acting like a plundering warlord, even if the people he slaughtered were not Israelites.

Living It Out

David's actions were borne of desperation and his decision was made without first seeking the will of God. He entered into an impossible alliance with Philistia and to maintain it had to slaughter many people. Any time we are faced with a desperate situation, we should seek God's guidance before acting. Otherwise, the unintended consequences of our actions may overwhelm us. Above all, we should have faith in God's ability to see us through our troubles without us having to take extreme measures and do things that are, at the least, unseemly.

Saul's Apostasy

1 Samuel 28:1–25

The Big Picture

The focus here turns back to Saul and to the last significant act of his life before his defeat in battle and death. It is a difficult passage; the interpretation of the events described is controversial. What is clear, however, is how disobedience to God leads to terrible apostasy, moral degradation, and a shameful ending.

Digging In

The Philistine Pentapolis evidently united all their forces for a decisive battle against Saul. This would be the first time that David would be expected to fight against the Israelites in full view of his new master, Achish of Gath. To make his expectations clear, Achish informed David that he and his men would be accompanying the Philistine army to the battle. David gave Achish the ambiguous answer, "Good, you will find out what your servant can do" (1 Sam. 28:2). To all appearances, Achish was so impressed that he made David his personal bodyguard. This may strike us as very strange, but actually it has long been common for kings to use foreigners and mercenaries as their personal guards. Unlike native troops, foreigners have no political alliances or personal relationships in the host country and will usually show high loyalty to the man who sponsors and pays them. We might speculate that David intended to betray Achish and change sides in the middle of the battle, but that is pure speculation. David was going to be in quite a bind; he would have Philistine soldiers all around him, and even if he turned against them and survived the fight, he had no reason to think that Saul would be well disposed to him.

Suddenly, however, the scene of the story shifts from David's interactions with Achish to the turmoil of Saul as he approached the battle. The text reminds us that Samuel was dead, but it adds the fact that Saul had removed mediums and spirits from the land (v. 3). The battle would take place in the vicinity of Mount Gilboa. This hill was located to the north, on the eastern edge of the Jezreel Valley and not far from the Jordan River and Sea of Galilee. From the slopes of Gilboa, Saul could look across the valley and see the Philistines encamped near Shunem, on the slopes of another hill (Mount Moreh) to the northwest. "When Saul saw the Philistine camp, he was afraid and his heart pounded" (v. 5). For all his faults, however, Saul was no coward. He was afraid because, seeing the unified Philistine army, he knew that catastrophic defeat for Israel was all but certain. Unlike David in the previous chapter, Saul sought an answer from God, but God did not respond. Saul's kingship had long since been repudiated by God, and yet, Saul had clung to power and even tried to kill the man he knew to be his chosen successor. As such, he had cut himself off from God.

We then come upon one of the strangest episodes of the Bible, Saul's encounter with the medium of En-dor (she is traditionally called the "witch of En-dor"). When Saul announced he wanted to find a medium, his staff curiously knew exactly where to find one (v. 7), even though Saul thought he had eradicated all mediums from the land. Saul disguised himself and set out with two men for En-dor, which was located on Mount Moreh north of Shunem, where the Philistines were camped. This meant that he had to go behind Philistine lines to get to her. He was truly desperate for some kind of supernatural message to give him guidance. The disguise and small escort were necessary both to fool the medium and to enable him to slip quietly past any Philistine patrol he might encounter.

Saul found the medium and sought her services. Since necromancy was a capital offense, the woman was naturally very cautious about taking on a new client. She had to be sure that the man before her was not an agent of Saul sent to entrap her. Little did she know that this man was Saul himself! Nevertheless, he swore in God's name that no harm would come to her—an ironic oath since he was now far from God (vv. 8–10).

From this point, the details of the story are straightforward but difficult to interpret. Saul asked to consult the spirit of Samuel, and when the woman saw Samuel, she suddenly realized that her client was Saul. Saul reassured her, and she told him that she saw Samuel as "a spirit form coming up out of the earth" in the form of an old man wearing a cloak (vv. 13–14). Saul somehow realized that it was indeed Samuel, and he knelt before the spirit. Saul told Samuel that he was facing a Philistine army and getting no answers from God. Samuel replied that God had repudiated Saul's kingship because of his disobedience and would give him no aid, that the battle would be lost, and that within a day Saul would be dead (vv. 15–19).

All of this raises many questions. We cannot possibly know how the woman suddenly recognized Saul or how Saul was able to be sure that the spirit was indeed Samuel, but we are left with much bigger questions. Did the woman really have the ability to summon spirits of the dead? Was the spirit that spoke to Saul really Samuel? Does this imply that necromancy is real and that gifted people really can speak with the dead?

The second question is the easiest to answer: The Bible calls the spirit "Samuel" (v. 16) and everything he said agrees with what Samuel believed and would have said. There can be little doubt that the spirit who spoke with Saul was indeed the deceased Samuel.

As to the first question, it is always possible that the woman was a charlatan like many modern spiritists. This was, however, a highly superstitious age, and she probably believed that she really could summon and speak with the dead. We might speculate that she was, knowingly or unknowingly, dealing with demonic entities, but the Bible is silent on that. In my view, the most likely explanation for this particular event was that God allowed (or caused) the spirit of Samuel to be present at that time. For us, the "success" of the medium of En-dor should be regarded as a one-time event for this unique occasion.

As to the third question: The episode does not in any manner legitimize necromancy or spiritism. The practice is forbidden (Lev. 19:26, 31; 20:6, 27; Deut. 18:11; Isa. 8:19–20). This was almost certainly an exceptional event, and exceptional events are not to be imitated or regarded as precedents. What Saul did was evil, and even if he got an answer (not the answer he wanted), the actions of an apostate king do not legitimize the practice.

The end of the narrative is somewhat touching. Saul had fallen into deep depression, but the woman showed him kindness and respect, giving him a very expensive meal (offering someone the fatted calf was a high honor indeed). In this, she gave respect to the king on the last day of his life. The narrative plainly portrays this as a generous act and an encouragement for Saul to face the coming day like a man. The biblical authors felt no need to vilify characters, making them out to be as evil as possible. The woman's practice of necromancy was evil, but the Bible does not shy away from recording when even an evil person does something honorable.

Living It Out

If we fall into disobedience and do not repent, everything will spiral out of control. Like Saul, we will become increasingly self-centered and even irrational. We will become highly inconsistent, at one point reacting in a way our Christian background has taught us to act, and at another time, blindly following our emotional fury. At the end, we will do something we once thought of as unspeakably evil. Saul knew that necromancy was wrong and had once tried to end it. On the last day of his life, he sought it out.

David's Avoidance of Treason

1 Samuel 29:1–11

The Big Picture

David comes to yet another moment of crisis: he is a member of the Philistine army coming to do battle against the Israelites! This is truly a "no-win" situation for him. Worse yet, from what we see in the text, David himself scarcely seems to realize what a bind he is in. Unless there is some intervention, David will have to make a terrible choice. The intervention does come, and from an unexpected source.

Digging In

Our narrative begins with an approaching battle. The geographical note, that the Philistines were at Aphek and the Israelites at the spring in Jezreel (1 Sam. 29:1), is confusing. In 1 Samuel 28:4, the Philistines were at Shunem on Mount Moreh and the Israelites were on Mount Gilboa. Both places are on the northeast edge of the Jezreel Valley, but Aphek is on the Sharon plain, about forty miles southwest of Shunem, and the city of Jezreel is close to the center of the Jezreel Valley. We can only conclude that the events of chapter 29 took place prior to the events of chapter 28. After the events of chapter 29, the armies moved to Shunem and to Mount Gilboa, and the events of chapter 28 took place.

The narrative of 1 Samuel 29:2–7 is straightforward. While at Aphek, the other Philistine lords became alarmed that David was in the middle of their army, and they did not trust him. Fearing he would turn against them at the height of battle, they demanded that Achish dismiss him and send him back. Achish, not wanting to cause conflict in the Philistine coalition, told David that he had to return to Ziklag.

The most vexing question in the narrative is why David protested so vigorously about being dismissed: "But what have I done? From the first day I entered your service until today, what have you found against your servant to keep me from going to fight against the enemies of my lord the king?" (v. 8). The animosity of the Philistine warlords gave him the perfect escape from his dilemma. He could avoid having to fight against the Israelites while not having to compromise his position before Achish. Thus, he could remain safely ensconced at Ziklag while awaiting news of the demise of Saul. One would think that David's most reasonable response would be to say, "Well, I am sorry they feel that way, but I suppose I can understand their concern," and then to get as far away from the battlefield as possible.

One might argue that David was intending to assassinate Achish and turn against the Philistines in the heat of the battle, thus gaining hero status for himself in the eyes of the Israelites. This would be a high-risk strategy, as nothing guaranteed that he would make it out of the Philistine camp alive, who would certainly in their rage turn all their power against him. Furthermore, had David's actions enabled Saul to survive the battle, the king's former behavior tells us that he would have quickly turned against David, killing him as treacherously as David had killed Achish. Furthermore, David had become the vassal of Achish. For him to turn against his lord in the midst of a battle would be, by the standards of the time, an act of inexcusable treachery. If David wanted to behave morally, he needed first to formally end the relationship before he could turn against Achish. To fail to do so would mark him in the minds of all his contemporaries, including the Israelites, as a dangerously amoral and utterly untrustworthy man.

Most importantly, the Bible never suggests that this was David's intent. The narrator almost certainly would not have skipped something as important as this. A typical way the Bible indicates the intent of someone is to report something like, "For David said in his heart, 'I will strike down the Philistine in the battle, and show myself to be for the Israelites and for Saul'" (for examples of the Bible describing a person's inner thoughts, see Gen. 17:17; Exod. 2:14; 2 Sam. 21:16; Esther 6:6). We see nothing like this in the account. We can only conclude that David had no such plans; indeed, it seems likely that he did not know what he was going to do.

How then do we explain David's words to Achish in 1 Samuel 29:8? An unfortunate aspect of David's character is that he was a fairly accomplished liar and actor. We saw this when he lied to Ahimelech, priest of Nob, resulting in a great massacre of the priests there (1 Sam. 21:1–22:19). We also saw how he feigned madness in his first encounter with Achish (1 Sam. 21:10–15) and how he later convinced Achish that he was raiding Israelite settlements, which was another lie (1 Sam. 27:10–12). The most reasonable explanation for David's words is that he got so caught up in his feigned role of Achish's faithful vassal that he played it to the hilt, showing outrage that anyone would doubt his loyalty to the Philistines. Behind all of this, we see the hand of God, who got David out of that awkward situation by means of the suspicion of the other Philistine lords. In short, David, in spite of himself, was saved by the hand of God.

We have already noted that biblical narratives tend to include episodes that parallel one another, and we have noted that this was the second time David fooled Achish (the first being when he pretended to be insane). It would seem that the Bible is pointing to certain flaws in David's character. These will become more pronounced as he becomes older, culminating in the Bathsheba affair.

But Achish, totally convinced that David was his loyal vassal, dismissed him from service on that day of battle. He had him depart as early as possible, as soon as it was light enough for David and his men to find their way out of the camp (1 Sam. 29:9–11). This was because

Achish did not want to arouse any distrust among his Philistine peers by having David be seen in the camp on the next day. David had to be well clear of the theater of battle before hostilities commenced.

Living It Out

The Philistine lords were justifiably suspicious of David, and their words were harsh and unyielding. Nevertheless, their demand that Achish dismiss David was his salvation from a hopeless dilemma. David was God's anointed, chosen to become Israel's king. We, as readers, are meant to see the hand of God behind this. Just as God delivered Abraham when he lied to the pharaoh about Sarah being his wife (Gen. 12:10–20), so also God saved David from the web of lies he had crafted and in which he was about to be ensnared. God chose both Abraham and David, and his plans would go forward in spite of human failings. For that, we should be grateful. How many of our mistakes has God had to overrule for us?

David's Victory over the Amalekites

1 Samuel 30:1–31

The Big Picture

Sometimes we all wander in the wilderness, our missteps having gotten us into a series of difficulties. In the previous reading, David was trapped by two bad options, either betraying his oath to Achish or fighting against Israel, and God, in his providence, delivered him by means of the suspicion of the Philistine lords. But David had still not been fully brought back to reality and to God. He needed a profound, palpable crisis to make him turn to God and get his priorities back in order. In this chapter, he faces such a crisis.

Digging In

David's troop made it back to Ziklag in about three days. They covered a significant distance, but most of it was in the relatively flat, coastal plain, since they could pass through Philistine territory unmolested. Still, it was a forced march, and the effort would take a toll on

David's men. Arriving at home, they discovered it burned out by the Amalekites and all of their families gone. Their wives and children were kidnapped and not killed; David's men presumably could have determined this from the fact that there were no corpses lying about. This was important, since it made rescue a possibility. David, of course, had slaughtered all the people in the settlements he had sacked. We should not think that the Amalekites acted out of mercy; they wanted prisoners to sell into slavery. At the same time, we cannot fail to notice the difference.

Of all the peoples David had plundered during his time at Ziklag (the Geshurites, the Girzites, and the Amalekites), the Amalekites were by far the most dangerous. They had been more or less at permanent war with the Israelites ever since they attacked them during Israel's exodus journey (Exod 17:8–16), and of course Saul had fought against them (1 Samuel 15). We read in this chapter how they moved about rapidly, on camels (v. 17). They lived as pirates of the desert, going from place to place and plundering as they went. The Israelites at this time fought entirely as infantry; significant cavalry or chariots did not become part of the Israelite army until Solomon "went down to Egypt" and bought horses (1 Kings 4:26–28; 10:28; see also Deut. 17:16). For this reason, it must have seemed to David's men that they had no chance of catching up with the Amalekites, and in their despair, they sat and wept (1 Sam. 30:4). More than weeping, they were ready to stone David to death. His involvement with the Philistines had so bound them to Achish that they had to go out to join his army marching to fight Saul, so that they had been forced to leave Ziklag undefended. Almost certainly, some of the men were already wondering about David's leadership, and this crisis nearly forced them into open rebellion.

But for David, the crisis had a salutary effect, bringing him to his senses. He first "found strength in the Lord his God" (v. 6), meaning that he turned back to God after having for so long made decisions on his own. He then asked the priest Abiathar to bring the ephod, a priestly vestment, meaning that he wanted to seek a word from God using the Urim and Thummim that the ephod carried. He asked if he could overtake the raiders, which was a reasonable question since he and his men were on foot, but the Amalekites rode camels. God replied that he would catch them and even save his people. It is not surprising that they could overtake the Amalekites; although the Amalekites could ride camels, they would drag their captive women and children along on foot, slowing the whole procession.

The Wadi Besor was one of the seasonal streams that crossed the barren region of the Negev, south of Ziklag. When they reached this spot, two hundred men, a full third of David's fighting force, were too weary to go on. Their exhaustion is attributable to the fact that they had just made a hard march from Aphek, where they separated from the Philistine army, to Ziklag. For these men, it had been too much, and David left them to watch over the equipment of the troops. The remaining four hundred, now with their kits considerably lightened, made more rapid progress after the Amalekites.

By good luck—or by the hand of God—they came upon an Egyptian slave who had been abandoned by his Amalekite master in the desert. Carefully reviving him with a small quantity of figs and raisins, and some water (too much food and water all at once would have been detrimental), they questioned him and found that he could lead them to one of their regular camp sites. When they arrived, they attacked the camp, but there was no real battle to speak of. The Amalekites were drunk and all of their leading men, who would have had first pick at the plunder, were incapacitated. The younger men of the Amalekites had their wits but were not prepared for an onslaught by the angry Israelites and fled as quickly as possible. Thus, David was able to recover the families of his men and also an enormous amount of booty, since the Amalekites had also raided Philistine towns (vv. 16–20).

David was once again behaving like a true leader. When some of the four hundred men who had made the march and killed the Amalekites demanded that nothing be given to those who guarded the supplies, David tactfully, but firmly, made it clear that this would not be his policy. Henceforth, troops who stayed back on guard duty would have an equal share with those who went out to battle (vv. 21–25).

In addition, David realized he had to stop playing at being Achish's vassal and prepare to lead Israel. He sent gifts from the plunder to leaders from the major towns of Judah (vv. 26–31), knowing that if he was to be accepted as the next king of Israel, he had to begin by making his own tribe, Judah, his base of support. It may be that he sent out the gifts after he had heard that Saul had been defeated and killed, marking the time for him to assume power. The town "Bethel" mentioned here (v. 27) is not the famous Bethel where Jacob encountered God (Gen. 28:10–19), in central Canaan. This was a smaller Bethel and located in Judah.

Living It Out

In this passage, David for the first time in a long time sought direction from God. He once again showed great qualities of leadership and realized that he had to take steps to secure his future among his own people. All of this came about as a result of the crisis he faced. If we do not respond to the gentle voice of God, he may call us back to himself and to our senses by trauma and pain. May we all learn to repent before we have to face such discipline.

Saul's Death

1 Samuel 31:1–13

The Big Picture

The book ends with the death of Saul. What are we to make of him? We have seen how his character changed and declined through the years of his reign, but we have also seen his dedication to fulfilling his mandate to lead Israel in their wars against their enemies. Clearly, he was a mixture of good and evil. Our reaction to Saul's life and death is a measure of our ability to make mature evaluations of people.

Digging In

Without giving us any specifics, verse 1 simply tells us that the Israelites and Philistines fought a battle and the Israelites lost. The fact that it was fought on Mount Gilboa, where Israel had encamped, suggests that the Israelites had taken up a defensive position on the hill and the Philistines attacked. Since the Philistines were willing to press their attack uphill, it may be that they had a numerical advantage; perhaps they outflanked the Israelites with their greater numbers, rolled them up, and put them to flight.

Verse 2 tells us, again very succinctly, that Saul's three sons were killed in the fighting. Even though the book elsewhere gives a fair bit of attention to Jonathan, it passes over in silence the desperate struggle of his last hour; we know nothing about how he fought and died. It does give us more information about Saul. He was wounded by archers and, seeing that the battle was lost and that he was about to be taken, he told his armor-bearer to strike him down rather than allow him to fall into enemy hands. Saul's concern was not just that they would torture him; the Hebrew implies that he thought they would humiliate him while they slowly killed him, exposing him by their maltreatment both to great physical pain and to public disgrace. He certainly preferred a swift death to that. Regardless of their dire situation, his armor-bearer, having always believed that the king's body was sacrosanct, could not bring himself to commit regicide, even when ordered to do so by the king himself. Saul, therefore, simply fell on his sword, a classic method of suicide in the ancient world. The armor-bearer did the same, and the Philistines' victory was complete (1 Sam. 31:3–6).

The battle had been a major engagement and a massive defeat for Israel, and Israelites in the towns and farms throughout the Jezreel Valley and surrounding hill country knew that they would be ravaged and plundered by the Philistine force. Taking what possessions and livestock they could, they fled across the Jordan River. Having suffered many defeats and setbacks at the hands of Saul, the Philistines had reversed the tide. The resumed their encroachment upon the Israelite territory, occupying land that would almost split Israel in half, with the Philistine-controlled Jezreel Valley sitting between Ephraim and Judah to the south and the territory around Galilee to the north.

The Philistines could not torment the living Saul, but they could abuse his corpse. They decapitated the body and hung his body on the wall of Beth-shan. This was a significant city to the east of Mount Gilboa; it occupied a hill directly above the west bank of the Jordan. The city is now a major archaeological site and national park in modern Israel. It has magnificent ruins, although most of these come from the later Greco-Roman city called Scythopolis. But the fact that the Philistines were able to penetrate this far, right up to a fortified city on the Jordan River, tells us how great their victory was and how much land they seized. Hanging his body on the wall of this prominent, elevated city showed all the Israelites that they had eliminated the king in whom Israel had placed all their hopes. They showed that they now had their boot on Israel's neck. The next leader of Israel would have a huge task before him.

In ancient warfare, as soon as a battle ended, the victors would send out heralds to proclaim their victory. People in their towns, hearing the good news, would eagerly await the return of the army and the plunder they would carry. Girls would come out and dance in the streets. Celebrating soldiers would set up a trophy on the battlefield, and the victors would send some of the plunder enemy armor to the temples of their gods as tokens of thanks. This is what is briefly mentioned in 1 Samuel 31:9–10, and it is also behind the opening words of David's lament over Saul and Jonathan: "The splendor of Israel lies slain on your heights. / How the mighty have fallen! // Do not tell it in Gath, / don't announce it in the marketplaces of Ashkelon, / or the daughters of the Philistines will rejoice, / and the daughters of the uncircumcised will celebrate" (2 Sam. 1:19–20). The celebrating of the Philistines left a bitter taste in David's mouth, as it did for all the Israelites. We note also that the first Philistine city David mentions in his lament is Gath, where David had spent much time as a vassal to Achish.

Saul's first victory was his deliverance of Jabesh-gilead, where Nahash the Ammonite had threatened to mutilate the men of the city (1 Samuel 11). The people of Jabesh-gilead did not forget Saul and what they owed him, and it so happened that Jabesh-gilead, just east of the Jordan River, was not too far from Beth-shan, where Saul's body was hung. In a daring, nighttime raid, they recovered Saul's body and those of his sons and brought them to their city. Having burned the bodies so that only the bones were left, they gave the remains a suitable resting place under a tamarisk tree and fasted in mourning over the deaths. Israelites did not practice cremation, and this was not a complete cremation since only the flesh was burned away while the bones remained intact. Their normal procedure was to allow the bodies to decay in a cave or secluded place and then inter the bones in the ground or a family tomb. Since Saul's body had been decapitated and abused, the

people of Jabesh-gilead probably felt it was best to hurry the process by
burning the flesh.

Living It Out

Saul and his sons died in fulfillment of the divine decree that
his crown was forfeit and could not be passed on to his offspring. But
he did not die ignobly; he faced the Philistines bravely and died with
their arrows piercing his body. Both Samuel and David wept over him
(1 Sam. 16:1; 2 Sam. 1:17). The book, ending with the tribute of the
men of Jabesh-gilead, acknowledges that there was much that was
heroic about him. We should not elevate any of our heroes too highly,
but we should also not condemn without qualification those who
sinned and failed. If we so rigidly divide people between good and evil,
we lack both maturity and grace, and we set ourselves up for failure and
disappointment.

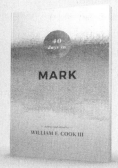